Let's go swimming

Colin Hardy

Hutchinson

London   Melbourne   Sydney   Auckland   Johannesburg

Message to the teacher

Let's Go Swimming is about the teacher and the pupil working together in an aquatic environment. From reading and using the ideas in this book it is hoped that you will gain a better understanding of swimming activities and their presentation, and that you will encourage your pupils to explore the wide range of swimming skills in an enjoyable and safe way. If you can inspire your pupils with a life-long interest in swimming, then you can be well satisfied.

Acknowledgements

I wish to thank my wife, Jennifer, for encouraging me in this project and for checking the draft copy. My two daughters, students from Loughborough University of Technology and the pupils of St. Botolph's Primary School, Shepshed and Shepshed High School for acting as subjects for the photographs. Also, my thanks to Peter Cullen, the illustrator, and to Ian Reynolds, Keith Pugh and Derek Blease for their photography. Cover photo reproduced by kind permission of Ian Reynolds.

Hutchinson Education
An imprint of Century Hutchinson Ltd
62–65 Chandos Place, London WC2N 4NW

Century Hutchinson Australia Pty Ltd
PO Box 496, 16–22 Church Street, Hawthorn,
Victoria 3122, Australia

Century Hutchinson New Zealand Ltd
PO Box 40–086, Glenfield, Auckland 10, New Zealand

Century Hutchinson South Africa (Pty) Ltd
PO Box 337, Bergvlei 2012, South Africa

First published 1989
© Colin Hardy 1989

Set in 10½/11pt Imprint by Hope Services, Abingdon
Designed by Robert Wheeler Associates
Printed and bound in Great Britain by
Scotprint, Musselburgh

British Library Cataloguing in Publication Data
Hardy, Colin A.
   Let's go swimming.
   1. Swimming. Teaching – Manuals
   I. Title
   797.2′1′07
ISBN 0 09 182266 1

Contents

1 *Why swim?* 5
A discussion of past and present attitudes towards swimming and the various reasons for wanting to swim. *5*

2 *Pre-lesson checklist* 7
Some fundamentals (e.g. buoyancy, mechanical principles) *7*
Some environmental and personal factors (e.g. water temperature, pool lay-out, hygiene) *12*
Water safety (e.g. rules) *14*
Artificial aids *16*
Crucial stages in learning to swim *19*

3 *First steps – make it enjoyable* 22
Confidence practices *22*   Game forms *26*
Early attempts at the strokes *29*

4 *Stroke development – keep it simple* 36
General notes *36*   Back crawl *37*
Front crawl *42*   Breast stroke *49*
Life saving kick *57*   Elementary back stroke *59*
Butterfly dolphin *62*   Side stroke *70*

5 Elementary diving – make it safe 73
Early practices 73 Plunge dive 78
Plain header 79

6 Water safety skills – get involved 81
Survival 81 Life saving 91
Expired air method of resuscitation 96

7 Application – make it active 103
Starting competitive swimming (e.g. starts, turns, schedules) 103 Life saving problems 118
More practices and the development of a game form 124

8 Lesson plans – get variety 128
A confidence lesson (non-swimmer) 128
An early stroke lesson (elementary swimmer) 131
A water safety lesson (more advanced swimmer) 134
A competitive swimming lesson (more advanced swimmer) 137
A fitness lesson (enthusiast) 139

Index 143

Why swim?

The excitement of a child swimming for the first time or the enjoyment and satisfaction of the elderly adult swimming easily through the water are heartwarming sights. From surveys carried out on sports participation swimming emerges as one of the most popular activities. The reasons for this popularity may vary, but it is a sport that costs little, caters for people of all ages and can be practised individually or in group situations.

Many teenagers and adults participate in sport for fitness purposes, but bruised ankles, blistered feet and strained backs can be the result of jarring movements in activities such as squash and jogging. With swimming, people can exercise without fear of minor injuries; joint mobility can be improved and the potential for sustained hard work is heightened because of the increased heart volume in the horizontal position.

Some participants enjoy the relaxation and freedom they find in the swimming pool. The relaxation comes from getting away from the stresses of everyday life and the freedom from moving silently in a world without gravity.

The competitive element is an important aspect of the sport for some swimmers. Being placed in an age-group or masters' competition may satisfy the better performers, while, for others, to achieve a given distance on a particular stroke may be enough.

If basic water safety practices are included in a swimming programme, not only are swimmers more likely to save themselves in an emergency, but they may be able to help others in difficulties should the need arise. Many drownings could be prevented if more people had a knowledge of rescues, tows and resuscitation.

Swimming is frequently recommended as a therapeutic exercise after injury or illness. The knee that is painful when walking may be exercised gently in the swimming pool without too much strain; the road to recovery may be a carefully structured swimming programme.

People with varying degrees of disability and impairment can also benefit from swimming. With the greater body support in water, less effort and strength is needed for movement, and many, confined to the wheelchair or bed in everyday life, can attain the upright position without help. A well-planned programme can ensure that objectives are within reach and that

6 Why Swim?

the learner feels a sense of achievement by continual successes. A further benefit is that the programme will contribute to organic and motor development.

From studies on infants it has been found that in the first few months of life the reflexes of breath control and swimming motions are quite strong when babies are submerged in water. Although these reflexes weaken and older infants do not find swimming an innate ability, they very quickly learn limb movements in the horizontal position. Nowadays swimming for babies is actively encouraged in many countries for health and safety reasons. Lessons in the swimming pool combined with basic water practices in the bath at home are all part of the 'parent–baby' swimming boom.

With the general emphasis in society on well-being and gaining life-time interests, there has been a tremendous increase in adult learn-to-swim classes. Adults are beginning to realise that failure or lack of opportunity in early life does not mean that swimming is closed to them forever. Although the general teaching strategy towards all non-swimmers is similar, certain aspects may have to be emphasised with the adult non-swimmer. To prevent embarrassment, adult classes should be timetabled separately. Each person's progress should be measured against own past performances rather than against other members of the group. The ease and control an adult shows when moving through water should be emphasised over speed. To allow for individual choice, a multi-stroke approach should be used, although backstroke tends to be popular with adults because the face is above the water and there are no real breathing problems. Explosive activities such as diving should not be stressed, and stroke adjustments may need to be made to cater for physical difficulties such as restricted shoulder mobility.

If people are to benefit from the sport of swimming, good facilities combined with an effective teaching organisation is essential. It can be the perfect sport for many and must be given every opportunity to develop.

Pre-lesson checklist

Some fundamentals

Buoyancy

Archimedes' principle states that when a body is fully or partially immersed in a fluid there is a vertical upthrust on the body equal to the weight of the fluid it displaces. By slowly walking down the steps of a swimming pool a person will feel the water exerting an upthrust on the body, and this will get stronger as more of the body is immersed. If the weight of the body is less than or equal to the weight of an equal volume of water, the body will float (i.e. the density of the body is less than or equal to the density of water). Although sinkers can be found among very muscular people, the majority can float when the lungs are inflated during normal ventilation. By inflating the lungs, the volume of the body increases and displaces more water, but, as the lungs are full of air, the increase in body weight is minimal and thus the effective density of the whole body is decreased. Other body factors such as bone, muscle and fat will also have a bearing on floating ability. Pieces of bone and muscle have a density greater than water, whereas the density of fat is less. Therefore, to float, the human body must have an overall density less than that of water (see Table 2.1).

The actual floating position of the human body will depend upon the distribution of fat and muscle, the size of the lungs, the general build of the person and the shape adopted. The upthrust of the displaced water acts through the centre of gravity of the displaced water and is known as the centre of buoyancy. The weight of the body thrusts downwards through its centre of gravity, and it is when the downward and upward thrust are equal and opposite that the human body will float. As humans vary in their distribution of muscle and fat, length of limb and size of lungs, and as the densities of body parts are not spread evenly, the centre of gravity will differ from person to person. Usually the centre of gravity will be below the level of the centre of buoyancy but its exact proximity will not be uniform in

8 Pre-lesson checklist

$$\text{Density} = \frac{\text{Mass}}{\text{Volume}} \quad \begin{array}{l} \text{kg/m}^3 \quad \text{(kilogrammes per cubic metre)} \\ \text{OR} \\ \text{g/cm}^3 \quad \text{(grammes per cubic centimetre)} \end{array}$$

To float – body density *less* than the density of water.

Table 2.1. Density table *(values are approximate)*

Material	g/cm³	
balsa wood	0.20	
cork	0.21	**Float**
fat	0.94	
human body (female)	0.97	
human body (male)	0.98	
water	1.00	
muscle	1.05	
bone	1.80	
aluminium	2.70	**Sink** *(some humans*
copper	8.90	*are sinkers)*
lead	11.30	

Note: The density of sea water is 1.03 g/cm³.

humans. If a person assumes a back floating position it is most likely that the legs will gradually sink as the centre of gravity will not be beneath the centre of buoyancy until a vertical position has been reached (Fig. 2.1). The closer the centre of gravity and the

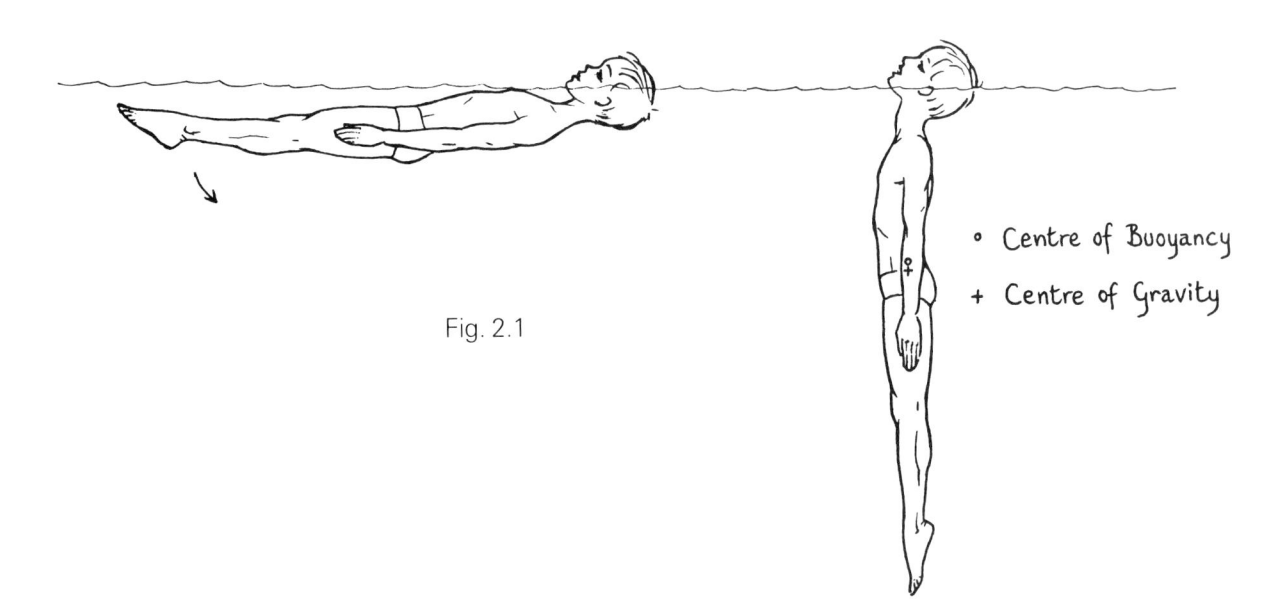

Fig. 2.1

∘ Centre of Buoyancy
+ Centre of Gravity

Fig. 2.2

centre of buoyancy, the quicker the floating position will be reached. By moving the arms from the side to above the head or by bending the legs (Fig. 2.2), the centre of gravity can be moved towards the head. Although there will also be a slight adjustment in the position of the centre of buoyancy, such limb movements tend to bring the centre of gravity and the centre of buoyancy closer together. However, it is unlikely that a person with a very muscular body and limbs will ever manage the vertical float, let alone a near horizontal position. The mushroom float, a closely tucked position on the front, is often used to check the floating ability of a person. By taking a deep breath in waist-high water and moving into the mushroom position the floater will find that the back will break the surface if the position is held for seven or eight seconds (Fig. 2.3).

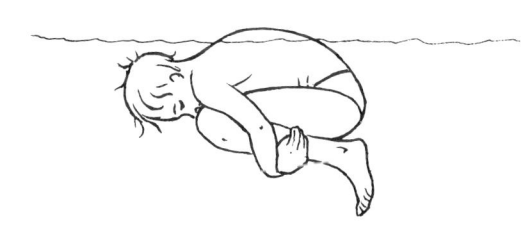

Fig. 2.3

Children tend to be more buoyant than adults and it would appear that this is the best time to teach swimming. It is undoubtedly an advantage if a person can assume the near-horizontal position easily, but there must also be the confidence to move into that position. Once the person can move into and out of the horizontal position safely and with confidence, the swimming movements can soon be developed. However, even if the person learning to swim is a poor floater or a sinker there is no reason to suppose that such a person will have difficulty in learning to swim. Artificial aids can be used to achieve the horizontal position and more emphasis may have to be placed on an efficient leg kick. If possible the buoyancy factor should be utilised, but the key factor is the person's confidence.

10 Pre-lesson checklist

Movement in water

According to Newton's First Law of Motion every body continues its state of rest or of uniform motion in a straight line unless acted upon by an outside force. If a person pushes away from the poolside in a front horizontal position, the friction of the water will cause a slowing down until the person stops. If the push-off is made in a more vertical position with the arms stretched out to the side, the stopping will be more abrupt because the body is badly streamlined (Fig. 2.4).

Fig. 2.4

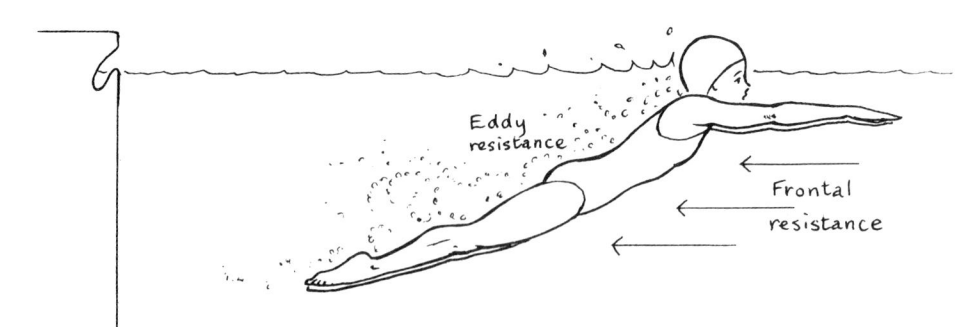

In swimming, a person must decrease this resistance and find ways of moving the limbs so that forward propulsion is obtained. Newton's Third Law of Motion says that to every action there is an equal and opposite reaction, and forward movement is therefore obtained by mainly pulling and pushing in the backward direction. From a study of top competitive swimmers it appears that, although the hands move in a backward direction, they do not move in a straight line (Fig. 2.5).

By moving the hands in curved pathways and at varying depths, a swimmer achieves propulsion. The continual change in the angle and direction of the hand into calm water gives the swimmer a better purchase on the water. This effectiveness can easily be tested by pulling the arm backwards in a zig-zag path and then in a straight line. It will be found that the hold on the water is soon lost in the latter movement.

When beginners learn the stroke techniques, it may be necessary to simplify the movements as the advanced strokes are not easy to acquire. For example, a straight arm pull in breast stroke swimming is much easier to learn than the high-elbow technique of the competitive swimmer. It will also be necessary to make the teaching points brief, as long descriptive instructions can be confusing. The teaching point 'kick with straight legs' emphasises a movement from the hips and avoids the complication of explaining that in back crawl the leg is bent at the bottom of the kick and straight at the top. As it is very difficult to keep a straight leg all the time there will be some bending at the knee automatically.

Some fundamentals 11

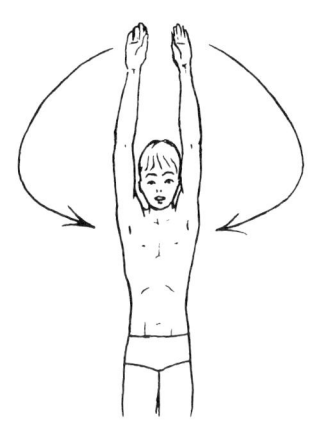

Fig. 2.5. (a) Breast stroke;

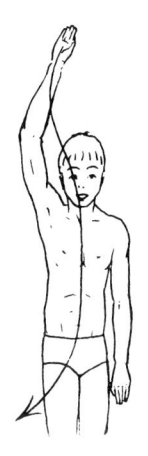

Fig. 2.5. (b) Front crawl;

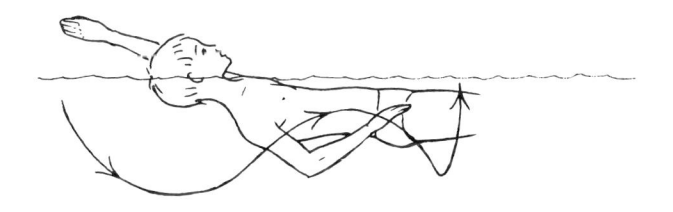

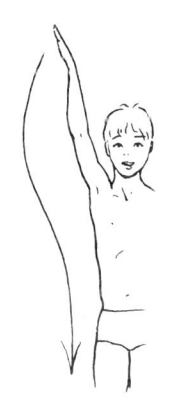

Fig. 2.5. (c) Back crawl;

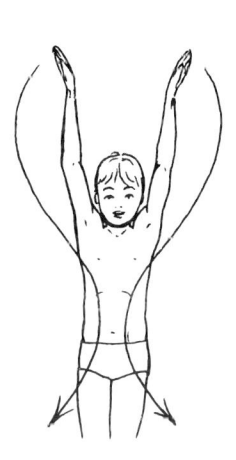

Fig. 2.5. (d) Butterfly.

Some environmental and personal factors

Water temperature

In a warm and comfortable swimming environment a swimmer can concentrate upon the task at hand. Although the ideal temperature for learning to swim cannot be specifically laid down, a temperature somewhere between 27 °C and 30 °C is generally acceptable. To avoid condensation in a swimming pool, the air temperature is usually a few degrees higher than that of the water temperature.

In most swimming pools the normal water temperature is usually slightly lower than 27 °C (e.g. 26 °C), although it may go as high as 32 °C for infant swimming classes. Younger children tend to lose heat very quickly and within six or seven minutes would soon be shivering in water temperatures of between 20 °C and 22 °C. In swimming pools where the water is cold, the learning time should be short and the practices vigorous.

Suitability of the pool

Pool design has changed dramatically over the last twenty years and pools can vary from the traditional rectangular shape to those in a landscaped setting with artificial waves. However, whatever the facilities, a responsible person should ask certain questions about the learning environment viz.:

- Are the shallow and deep ends of the pool clearly marked?
- Is there a large shallow water area?
- Does the water gradually get deeper or is there a sudden increase in depth?
- Is it possible to work across the pool?
- Does the pool have a rail or trough to hold on to?
- How high is the pool side from the water?
- Can artificial aids be used in the pool?
- Is there a designated diving area?
- Are the toilets clearly marked?
- Are there lifeguards on duty?
- Are the swimming pool rules and regulations posted on a noticeboard (Fig. 2.6)?

Hygiene

There appear to be standard procedures for all people who intend to enter a swimming pool. If these procedures are dealt with in a logical order an individual would carry out the following routine:

Some environmental and personal factors 13

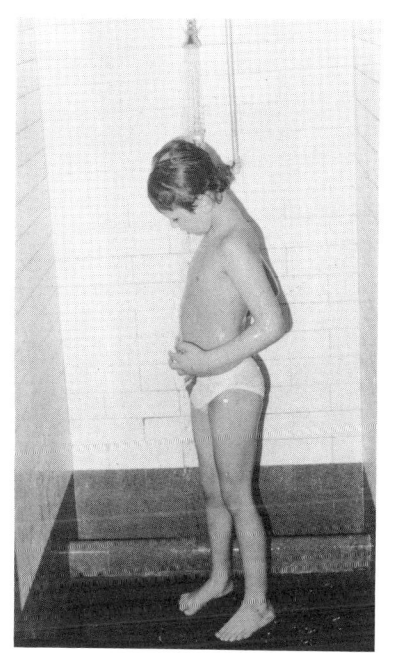

Fig. 2.6

Fig. 2.7

Routine	Notes
1. Arrange your clothing tidily in a cubicle or locker	– You can soon lose things
2. Blow your nose on a handkerchief before parting with your clothing	– If you have a cold or catarrh, you should not be here
3. If you are chewing gum or you have a sweet in your mouth get rid of it	– You can soon choke if you eat while swimming
4. Go to the toilet	– It is better to go before the lesson rather than interrupt it later
5. Take a shower (Fig. 2.7)	– Get rid of any dirt from your body, limbs and hair
	– Do not swim with open sores
6. Wash your feet thoroughly in the footbath	– If you have any foot infection (e.g. verruca), do not swim, but go and see your doctor
7. If you have long hair, put on a bathing hat or tie at the back if it is an acceptable practice in that pool	– Long hair can soon cover the face and cause breathing problems

SWIM

8. Take a shower after swimming	– These measures help to prevent infection
9. Dry yourself paying particular attention to the parts of the body that can easily be be missed (e.g. between the toes)	
10. Wash your swimming costume thoroughly	

Water safety

Drowning is one of the leading causes of accidental death in many developed countries. The figures that are produced by National Life Saving Bodies do not include the many situations where people were rescued, and thus do not adequately reflect the extent of the problem. With the increase in aquatic facilities, it is becoming even more crucial for people to become aware of the preventive measures that can be taken.

Swimming pool

Procedures	*Notes*
1. Walk along the pool side	– You can slip if you run
2. Co-operate with others to make the pool a safe place	– If you push or duck one another it can lead to an accident
3. Obey signals from the lifeguard or teacher	– The lifeguard may be indicating that you are swimming into a diving area
4. Use aids under supervision	– Certain aids are not sufficiently supportive for deep water practices – Fins can flick others in the eyes
5. Swim short distances underwater after taking one breath only	– Too many deep inhalations followed by swimming long distances underwater can lead to unconsciousness
6. Jump or dive into the water when it is clear of other swimmers	– You could hit somebody as you enter or as you re-surface
7. Dive into deep water only	– You can injure yourself seriously by diving into shallow water
8. Swim in that part of the pool that reflects your ability	– If you have just started to swim keep to the shallow end

9. Know the rescue equipment that is available in the pool	– Are there:
	    long reaching poles?
	    life-buoys?
	    heavy ropes?
	    emergency telephones?
	    pieces of first aid equipment?

10. Know what is expected of you in a class situation	– You enter when you are told – You stay in the area allocated to you – You must always get out of the water before being dismissed to the changing rooms
11. Know what is expected of your teacher in a class situation	– The teacher should always be on the pool side – The teacher should not put you into a crowded pool – The teacher can carry out emergency procedures

Open water

Procedures	Notes
1. Bathe at the seaside under controlled conditions	– You bathe in the area between the red and yellow flags – Do not bathe when the red flag is flying
2. Read the notices	– Notices usually give advice to bathers and they are not to be used as hanging pegs
3. Check that there are other people close by as you bathe	– Help is readily available if you get into difficulty
4. Swim close to and parallel with the shore	– If you swim too far out fast running currents can take you into the tidal stream
5. Leave the water if you feel chilled and/or start shivering	– Even the strongest swimmer can get cramp in cold water – Swimming too long in cold water can lead to hypothermia
6. Surf only in reasonable conditions	– Heavy surf can soon throw you off balance and wind you – If the beach is crowded you may collide with other bathers
7. Enter the sea with care	– Chasing a beach ball can take you into deep water – A run and a dive can be dangerous in unknown depths
8. Keep well away from boats	– You can easily be hit and perhaps caught up in the propellers of a power boat
9. Make sure that you do not swim immediately after a meal	– If you have a heavy meal before swimming, you may vomit and this can cause breathing problems
10. Keep away from the water if you have been drinking alcohol	– If you have been drinking alcohol your judgement will be impaired
11. Swim in closely supervised and known waters	– You may not get help in a secluded spot – It can be dangerous to swim near bridges, piers and wrecks as there can be treacherous currents – Ponds, gravel pits, lakes, canals, rivers can vary in depth, be polluted and contain rubbish and obstructions – Mud, soft sand, sandbanks, weeds, crumbling and slippery edges are all hazards in or near water – The flow of water from inlet and outlet pipes can drag you under

16 Pre-lesson checklist

Artificial aids

Many types of artificial aids are worn by weak swimmers and non-swimmers. The aid gives the learner the confidence to achieve the near-horizontal swimming position and to concentrate upon the propulsive movements of the arms and legs.

In any swimming session it is not advisable to use the aid continuously, as the learner still needs to build up confidence and control without any support. A lesson that combines artificial aid practices with gliding movements without aids would be the most effective.

As learners gain in confidence with their aids and start to move around, it is essential that the working area is roped off. Without such a preventive measure being taken it is quite easy to drift into deeper water (Fig. 2.8).

Make sure that any aid fits the learner properly so that it does not slip off and check that any plugs are pushed in firmly (Fig. 2.9).

Fig. 2.8

Arm bands: these are a favourite aid with younger children. They can move their arms easily and obtain reasonable support. With adults the arm bands do not support so well and may be more appropriate once they start swimming.

Ring: this aid can give adequate support to both children and adults. There can be some restriction on the arm movements, but it does allow the learner to concentrate upon ways of using the limbs for propulsive purposes.

Swim belt: this is an extension of the ring. The polystyrene blocks can be removed as the learner's confidence grows. A similar aid is a swim suit and this is ideal for the timid learner.

Fins: these can be used effectively by all learners, but their use must be controlled. The fins can easily flick into the face of another participant, and collisions may occur because of the extra speed that can be gained. If fins are used it should be under carefully controlled conditions; the working area should be roped off from other swimmers and the movement across the pool should be of a set pattern.

Kick board: the board can be used with other aids (e.g. the ring) to improve the leg kick. With children a polystyrene float can be used but this does not always give the adult ample support (Fig. 2.10).

Fig. 2.9 ▲ and Fig. 2.10

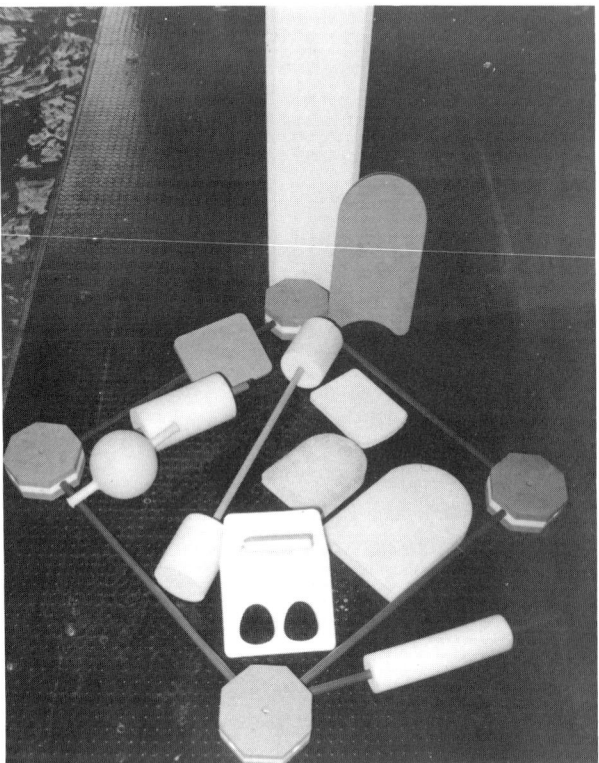

Fig. 2.11

Fig. 2.12

Other aids: as the learner starts to swim, training aids can be used to give variety to the lesson. Pull-buoys, hand paddles, tubes, drag belts and rings, hand weights and kicking devices are the types of aid used by the swimmer (Figs. 2.11 and 2.12).

Goggles: many learners see the competitive swimmers with their goggles and immediately regard them as an essential part of swimming equipment. If learners do find that their eyes are sensitive to swimming pool water they may feel happier wearing goggles. However, if goggles are used, certain precautions must be taken:
1. Take care in putting the goggles on and taking them off (there have been eye injuries).
2. Make sure that the goggles fit properly and are waterproof (you may have to try several types of goggles).
3. Try and avoid using goggles with younger children as they do not always fit a very small face satisfactorily.
4. Take each case individually.

Snorkel and mask: these aids give the learners the opportunity to breathe and look around under water. As with the fins, the equipment should be used under controlled conditions only.

Crucial stages in learning to swim

There has been much discussion over the years as to the most effective way of teaching the beginner. It has been suggested that a multi-stroke approach tends to be more succesful than that of teaching a single stroke, and that a block swimming course seems to produce better results than the traditional weekly lesson. The teacher–pupil relationship is an important factor and some teachers get good results irrespective of the teaching method. Artificial aids tend to help non-swimmers in the early stages, but they should not be overused.

Some writers have looked for relationships between psychological and physical measures of non-swimmers and learning to swim and they have found several influencing factors. A positive attitude and the ability to relax appear to be of some importance, and out-going children tend to learn quicker than the more introverted ones. There is some relationship with physical ability, and as children get older and stronger there is a better chance of learning to swim. Floating ability varies with age and sex and may have a greater bearing on the swimming position in the stroke development stage than on early attempts at swimming.

Fig. 2.13

However, the one factor that may have a profound influence on learning to swim is fear of water.

If persistent non-swimmers are asked why they have never learned to swim, the majority of them will say that they are afraid of water. In many cases, the fear stems either from one very unpleasant experience in water or a number of minor ones. With this in mind, it is important to associate water with pleasant and enjoyable feelings.

In learning to swim, individuals have to go through a number of crucial stages irrespective of age, background, teaching method and organisation. Some non-swimmers move through these stages very quickly, others take much longer, and some find that one particular stage causes special difficulties.

STAGE 1

> My first visit to the swimming pool is an enjoyable one.

Did you find the water warm?
Was everybody helpful?
Are you clear about the pool lay-out?
Do you want to come back again?
(Fig. 2.13)

STAGE 2

> I can walk around the shallow end of the pool without help.

Can you slide your feet along the bottom of the pool?
Can you use your hands to maintain balance?
Can you walk forwards, backwards and sideways?
Are you keeping your shoulders below the water surface?
Is it fun?

STAGE 3

> With my artificial aids I can propel myself in a back and front horizontal position, and I can regain my feet.

Can you find different ways of moving your arms and legs?
How far can you go?
Is it easy to get your feet back on the bottom of the pool?
Is it easy to move into the horizontal position?

STAGE 4

> I can glide to the pool side and I can regain my feet.

Can you get your legs up before you touch the wall?
Did you get to a near horizontal position?
Is it easy to get your feet back on the bottom of the pool?

Crucial stages in learning to swim

STAGE 5

| I can glide, kick and pull several times before touching the pool side. |

Did you get your legs up?
Did you feel yourself pulling?
What arm and leg movements did you use?
You are now swimming!

STAGE 6

| I can push away from the pool side, swim 5 metres and regain my feet. |

Did you keep your arms and legs going?
What stroke did you use?
Did you manage to breathe?
Did anybody see you swim the 5 metres?

STAGE 7

| I can swim 10 metres on a recognised stroke? |

Did you keep close to the water surface?
Did you use controlled arm and leg movements?
Did you breathe regularly?
Are you ready to improve your swimming ability?
You have achieved something that will be with you for the rest of your life!

Note: language to be adjusted for different age-groups.

3 First steps – make it enjoyable

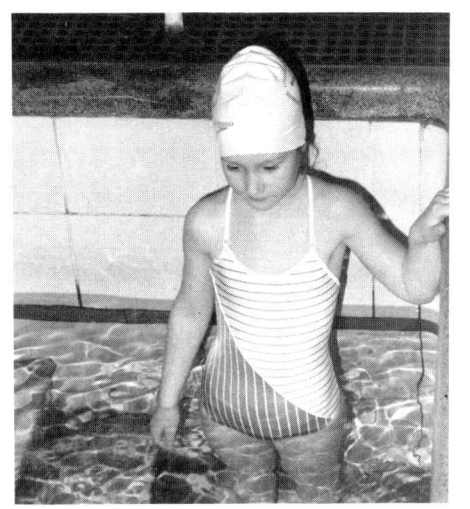

Fig. 3.1. (a)   Fig. 3.1. (b)

Confidence practices

Enjoyment in the early stages of learning to swim will entice learners back to the swimming pool. The first session must be an experience that the learners want to repeat as soon as possible.

Along with this enjoyment factor must go that of safety. From the very start organise a partner system whereby two learners stay close together and keep an eye on each other. In addition, place a lane rope across the pool to indicate the learners' working area.

Entry

There are several ways of entering the water and these may be tried out at different times during the early lessons. The simplest way is to walk down the swimming pool steps holding onto the side of the pool (Fig. 3.1). Some learners will do this quickly, others will enter more warily, and some may even need additional verbal persuasion. At this stage do not rush the learners but allow them to proceed at their own rate. The more confident ones will soon be sitting on the edge of the pool, holding onto the bar or trough with an underhand grip, and then slipping and turning towards the side as they enter the water (Fig. 3.2). The first hand will stay in contact with the side all the time and the second hand will take hold of the bar or trough as the turn is made into the water. At a later stage of development, learners will crouch down by the edge of the pool, with toes gripping the side, and grasp the hands of partners. They will then jump into the pool maintaining contact with their partners all the time (Fig. 3.3). Eventually, learners will be able to jump into the pool unaided (Fig. 3.4). These slipping in and jumping practices can only be done if the learners can place their feet on the bottom of the pool.

Walking

Once the learners are in the water they should hold the side of the pool and slide their feet along the bottom of the pool. If the knees are lifted too high the upthrust and the general sway of the water

Fig. 3.2. (a)

Fig. 3.3. (a)

Fig. 3.2. (b)

Fig. 3.3. (b)

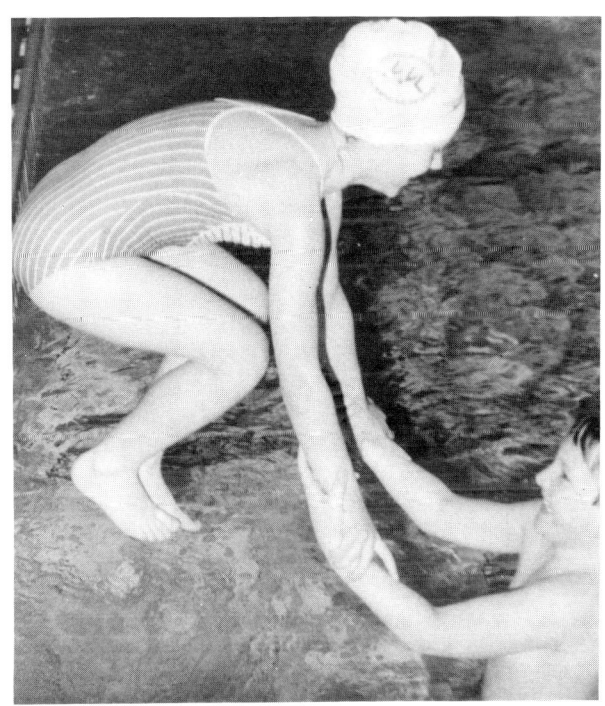

24 First steps – make it enjoyable

can unbalance them. The learners can be asked to walk, not only forwards, but backwards and sideways, with a variety of walking movements.

Can you:
- imagine you are ice-skating?
- lead with one foot all the time?
- walk with your feet turned outwards?
- walk with your feet turned inwards?

As the learners become more confident in the water, they may walk holding their partners' hands and, later, without any help at all. Once the learners are able to move without support the practices can be made more varied.

Can you:
- walk diagonally across the pool?
- walk and use arm movements?
- try different arm movements?
- work the arms together?
- work the arms separately?
- pull and recover keeping the arms under the water?
- pull and then recover the arms over the water?

Feet off the bottom of the pool

As progress is made, the skill of taking the feet off the bottom of the pool and then replacing them will have to be acquired. The first stage is to hold the side of the pool, walk one or two paces up the wall and then walk down again. Then, the learners can walk up the wall, move sideways along the wall and then walk down. The next stage is to grasp over the bar or trough and place the elbows firmly against the wall. By pushing the elbows into the wall the legs will rise (Fig. 3.5). To regain the feet, push down with the hands, raise the head and tuck the legs; once the feet are beneath the body, stretch the legs. Another hold that can be used is where one hand grasps over the bar or trough and the other is placed beneath with the palm against the wall and fingers pointing downward. With this hold, the legs can be lifted by pushing against the wall with the bottom hand (Fig. 3.6).

As water will certainly splash into the learners' faces in these early practices, they should practise blowing it away. By placing the mouth near to the surface they can blow bubbles into the water. By now, some learners may be putting their heads under the water surface quite happily and so for them there is no need to practise blowing as a special activity.

In these early stages, learners should be told not to rub their eyes if water goes into the face. Rubbing the eyes can cause irritation and lead to a redness and soreness.

The entry, walking and feet-raising practices can all be carried out without insisting that the head is placed under the water surface. Any insistence on getting the face wet may cause stress and eventual fear of water.

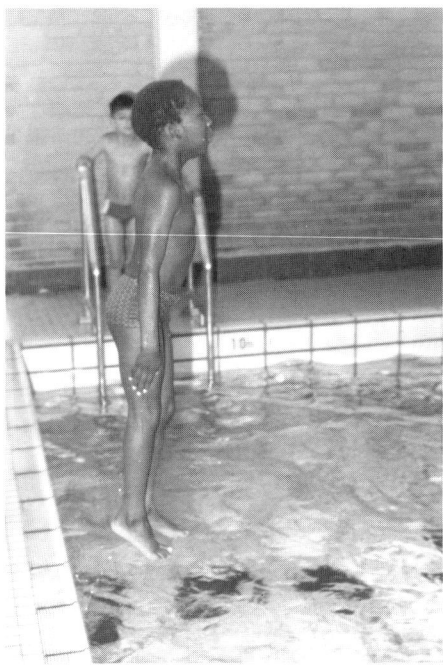

Fig. 3.4

Confidence practices 25

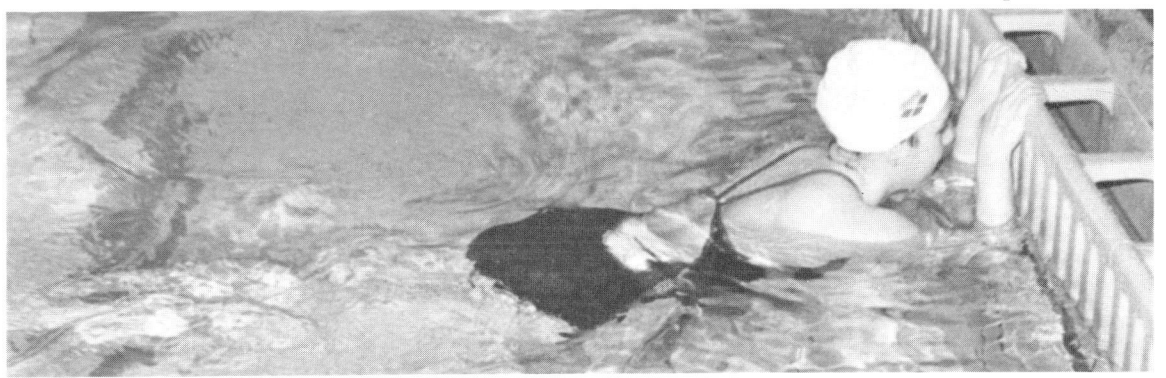

Fig. 3.5

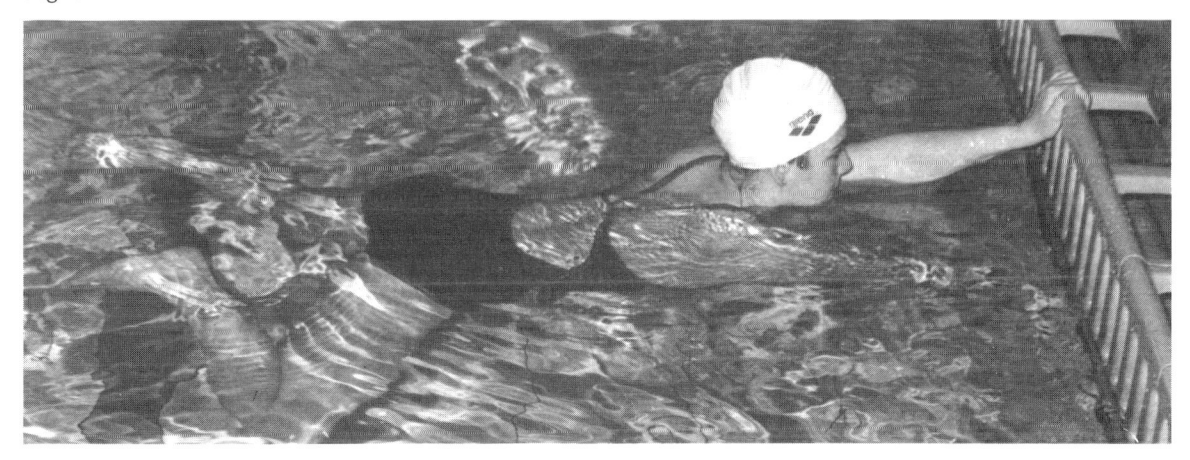

Fig. 3.6

With adults all these practices are still relevant, although certain adjustments in organisation and presentation may be necessary. They may prefer to practise in adult classes where members of the public are excluded; this may prevent embarrassment if difficulties are encountered. More time may have to be given to each practice; stiff shoulder, hip and ankle joints can restrict the range of limb movement and slow down the speed of progress. Whether the reason for not being able to swim is a lack of opportunity or unsuccessful earlier attempts, adults are usually well-motivated individuals. Safe and successful experiences at this stage in the learning programme will build up the confidence needed to attempt the stroke practices.

With less confident learners a ring or similar support can be worn while performing the practices. With a very timid learner it may be necessary for the teacher to go into the water. However, this should not take place in a swimming session with other learners; a separate lesson should be arranged so that all attention can be given to ensure there is no stressful experience. With the less confident and the timid, progress will be slower at first, but success, no matter how small, should be praised in order to help build up confidence.

In some teaching pools the water is shallow enough for the

26 First steps – make it enjoyable

learners to assume a horizontal position and place their hands on the bottom of the pool. In this environment arm and leg movements may be attempted while lying in the front or back positions.

Can you:
- pull yourself forward on your front?
- move feet first while on your front?
- move head first on your back?
- move feet first on your back?
- move using your arms alternately?
- move using your arms together?
- kick your legs up and down?
- kick your legs backwards and forwards?
- move kicking your legs alternately?
- move kicking your legs together?
- move kicking your legs and pulling with your arms?

In swimming pools where the learners are too small to stand on the bottom of the pool, an aid will have to be used. Practices could still be done holding the side of the pool, although horizontal and vertical positions would be achieved without touching the bottom. Movement of the arms and legs will be developed, using instructions similar to those in the shallow teaching pool, with the addition of trying all movement in both vertical and near-horizontal positions. To give all learners the opportunity to experience a prolonged horizontal position, a specific part of a lesson could be set aside for practising with aids. As there are many swimming aids, allow learners to try all types for variety and to adjust to slightly differing support positions.

There are many instances of babies swimming in pools before they can walk. However, the baby's pleasure and satisfaction from being in water will have already been developed at bath time in the home. For example, the bath should be filled with pure water, of a specified temperature, and all toys should be washed and disinfected. It is also recommended that the immediate family should act as teacher and helper, and that the lessons should be a regular time each day. Nowadays, baby and parent classes are provided regularly by local community facilities, but those using them should check for hygienic conditions, trained teaching staff and carefully graded and organised programmes.

Game forms

Game forms for learners with or without supportive aids are based upon the skills acquired in the confidence work. The objective is to get the learners to perform tasks that are fun without being dangerous. The key to this work is to get the learners involved without being competitive. If a competitive element is introduced it can lead to hurried, uncontrolled movements that are unsafe. As with the confidence practices, a lane rope should be placed across the pool to establish the learners' working area.

Walking

Walk hand in hand with a partner
Can you:
- walk holding with one hand?
- walk holding with two hands?
- walk forwards, sideways and backwards?
- move in a circle?
- keep changing direction?
- walk back to back?
- keep in time with your partner's movements?

Walk behind your partner
Can you:
- copy your partner's movements?
- keep hold of your partner's waist (Fig. 3.7)?
- walk as one?
- imagine that you are a train?

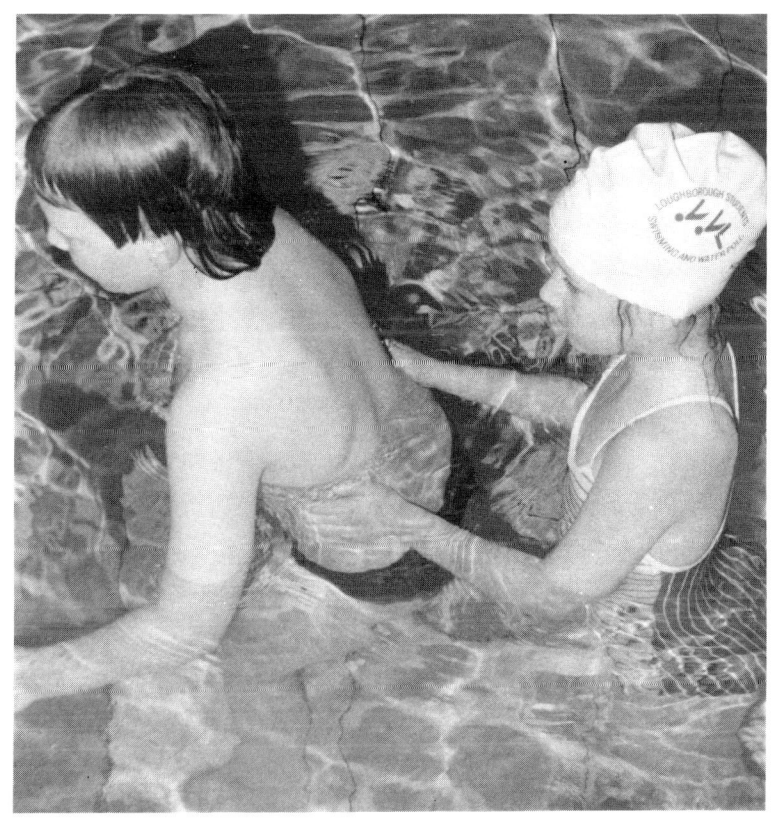

Fig. 3.7

Many of these movements can also be done in groups of three and four, but it is important to match the groups carefully. If a nervous learner gets involved with a more confident and active group who are continually splashing water around, that learner may lose confidence.

Play with a ball

In public swimming sessions, balls and other toys are often prohibited because such game forms can interfere with other swimmers and cause accidents. However, as many learn-to-swim classes take place in conditions specifically for learners, the use of equipment is often acceptable as long as it can be strictly controlled.

Balls may be of different sizes but they must be soft and large enough to be caught with ease. A hard ball hitting the face can be painful, and too many unsuccessful catching attempts may cause frustration rather than enjoyment.

Individual practices

Can you:
- push the ball along with your hands?
- push the ball along with your body?
- push the ball along with your nose, chin or forehead?
- move the ball along without touching it?
- keep the ball clear of the water?
- walk and pass the ball from hand to hand?
- pass the ball round your body?
- put the ball under the water and then let it go?

Pair practices

Can you:
- catch the ball from your partner's throw (Fig. 3.8)?
- make more than ten throws without the ball hitting the water?
- throw with your right hand?
- throw with your left hand?
- throw with both hands?
- head the ball to your partner?
- walk and pass the ball to each other?
- walk and hold the ball between your bodies?
- throw the ball into a hoop held flat in the water by your partner?
- throw the ball through the hoop held upright by your partner?
- pass a ball through a hoop that is held flat in the water by your partner?
- push the ball under your legs?

Group practices

Groups of three or four learners of a similar confidence level can practise throwing and catching skills in circles and in straight

Fig. 3.8

lines. All practices can be done in a stationary position or when moving.

Hoop activities

Individual practices

Can you:
- get into and out of a floating hoop (Fig. 3.9)?
- push the hoop underwater and step out of it?
- hold the hoop and walk along inside it?
- spin a floating hoop on the water surface?
- stand on the hoop?

As with the ball activities the hoop practices can be carried out in pairs and in groups. By combining walking, ball and hoop activities many other practices can be invented.

Equipment other than balls and hoops is available for learners (e.g. quoits) and it is really up to the teacher to develop a varied programme along the lines suggested. Enjoyment comes from how you use the equipment and not because it is available!

Putting the head under the water

As long as the learners have grown in confidence it may now be time to suggest some 'head under' practices. However, do remember that the learners who appear to do the early practices with ease but lose their smiles immediately water goes into the face should not be forced to place their heads under the water. Observe these learners carefully and wait until they show very little reaction to water splashing into the face.

Hold the side

Can you:
- blow bubbles on the water surface?
- blow bubbles under the water?
- open your eyes under water?
- crouch down under the water?
- see your partner under the water?
- get out of your floating hoop by going under the water?
- touch the bottom of the pool with your hand?

In the early attempts at the strokes 'head under' practices can be done away from the pool side, but, by then, the learners will have a much greater control over the water environment.

Fig. 3.9

Early attempts at the strokes

In the early attempts encourage all types of leg and arm actions, and their practice in moving with and without aids.

Gliding

Learners stand facing the pool side at a distance just over arm's length. The arms are stretched along the surface, the chin is on the water and the feet are placed in the lunge position; the body is then driven towards the pool side. Some learners will make contact with the side before the feet have left the bottom of the pool but this is only to be expected with the less confident ones. As confidence grows and the skill is perfected, learners will be able to glide in the horizontal position for short distances. From the very start emphasise the drive forwards and discourage any up and down movements.

The time when learners lose contact with the pool bottom and are still moving towards the side is a crucial stage in learning to swim. Although the distance will be increased as the performance improves, it must be remembered that it is the force of the drive that is giving the movement and not a swimming action.

As the learners master this important stage in stroke development other variations can be included:

Can you:
- keep your chin in contact with the water all the time?
- stretch your toes before touching?
- get your legs together before touching?
- kick before touching?
- pull before touching?
- kick and pull before touching?
- drive away from the pool side to a partner?
- push to the side holding a float?

Hold the side and practise leg actions

Can you:
- circle your legs?
- circle your legs with your feet turned out?
- kick your legs up and down with bent legs?
- kick your legs up and down with straight legs (Fig. 3.10)?
- kick up and down with legs together?
- kick up and down with pointed toes?

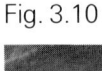

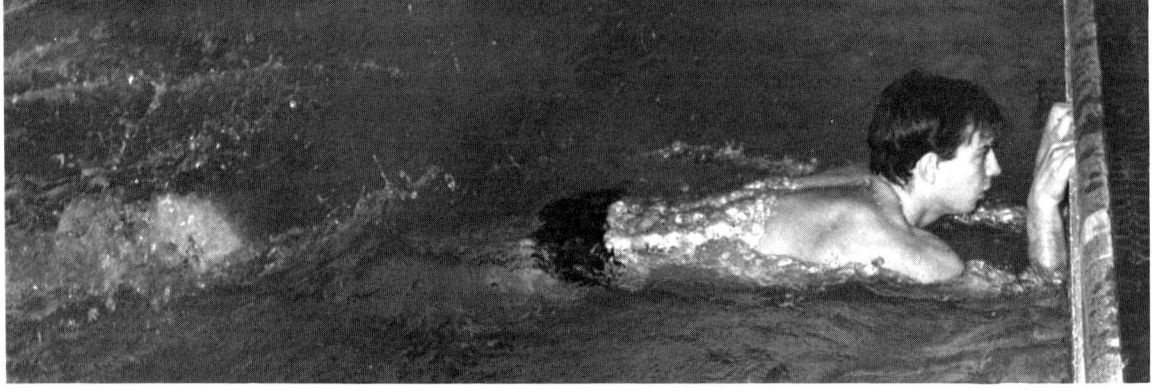

Fig. 3.10

Early attempts at the strokes 31

Fig. 3.11 left and Fig. 3.12

The learners can practise these leg actions in a back horizontal position by grasping over the bar or trough with straight arms extended to the side (Fig. 3.11) or bent over the shoulders (Fig. 3.12). It is not easy to achieve a horizontal position but it will be an introduction to the back strokes.

Work with supportive aids

If some of the time is spent on developing effective kicking and pulling actions, learners will start getting the sensation of movement in water. As long as the learners are old enough, such words as recovery, simultaneous and alternate can be explained in swimming terms. With younger children explanation and demonstration will have to go hand in hand.

Can you:
- pull yourself along with fingers open?
- pull yourself along with fingers closed?
- move using both hands together?
- move using one hand?
- pull with straight arms?
- pull with bent arms?
- feel the pressure against the palm of your hand?
- recover your arms alternately?
- recover your arms together?
- recover your arms through the water?
- recover your arms over the water?

If the learners still retain the supportive aids and hold a float, different leg actions can also be practised. The float should be

32 First steps – make it enjoyable

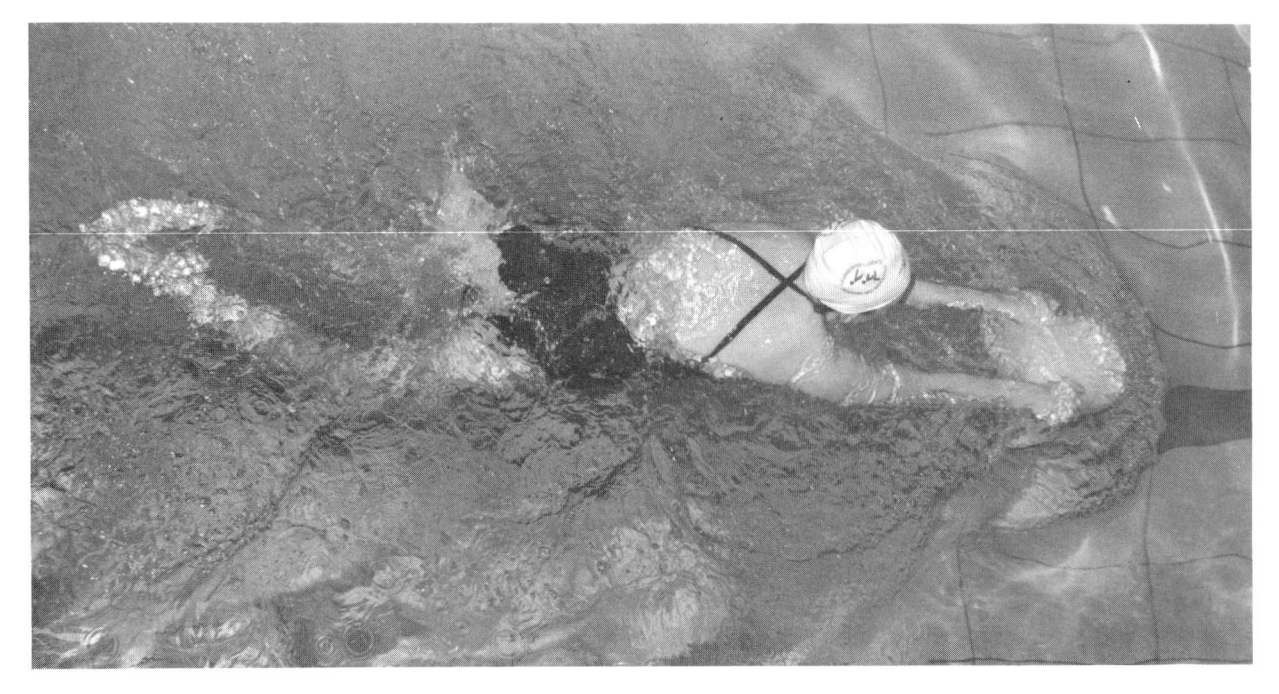

Fig. 3.13 ▲ and Fig. 3.14

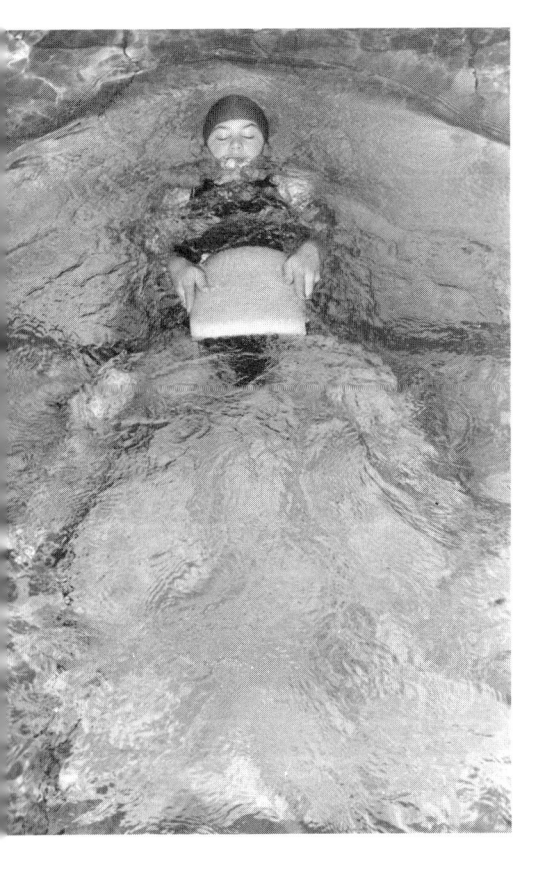

held at the sides and half-way along; the fingers will be placed beneath the float and the thumbs on top (Fig. 3.13). The leg actions that were attempted while holding the side can now be tried while holding the float. The main difference is that the learners will now experience movement.

If the learners turn onto their backs and hold the float above the hips (Fig. 3.14) the leg actions can still be attempted. Some learners find that they can perform the actions better when they can see their legs. There is also the point that the face is kept reasonably clear of the water, and they may find that they can concentrate on the actions without the worry of being continually splashed in the face.

The work with artificial aids can be developed by trying different combinations of leg and arm actions. These actions can be done in both the front and back lying positions.

By offering a mixture of these practices, the learners will soon be travelling short distances in the water. At this stage it is not the stroke that is important but the ability to use the arms and legs in a way that produces propulsion. There are several questions that learners should be constantly asked at this stage:

'Can you FEEL the water with your hands?'
'Have you POINTED your TOES?' (for crawl type movements)
'Have you turned your FEET OUTWARDS?' (for breast stroke type movements)

If learners can gain this awareness with the hands and this control of the feet, stroke development will be much easier.

Regaining the feet from front and back gliding movements

Once the learners start to swim short distances parallel to and away from the pool side, regaining the feet effectively is essential for safety and confidence.

A quick revision of the practices: 1. raising and lowering the legs while holding on to the bar or trough; and 2. gliding to a partner and regaining the feet should be carried out. The learners are then told that to regain their feet from a front gliding movement they have to pull down with the hands, lift the head and tuck the legs; once the legs have been brought beneath the body the learners reach for the bottom of the pool with their feet (Fig. 3.15). In attempting this for the first time the learner should glide towards a partner and try and regain the feet before making contact; if the learner finds any difficulty in regaining the feet, the partner can help.

Fig. 3.15

Regaining the feet from a back gliding movement is the next step. In the first instance the back glide can be made to a partner who pushes the head and shoulders forwards and upwards as the learner tucks and then stretches the legs. When the learner attempts this for the first time alone, a partner should be available just in case help is needed. Once the back gliding movement is achieved, the arms are brought in a bent position towards the shoulders and then swept downwards and backwards towards the feet; simultaneously the head and trunk are brought forwards and upwards and the legs are tucked. As the legs are brought beneath the body, the learner stretches the legs and reaches for the bottom of the pool (Fig. 3.16).

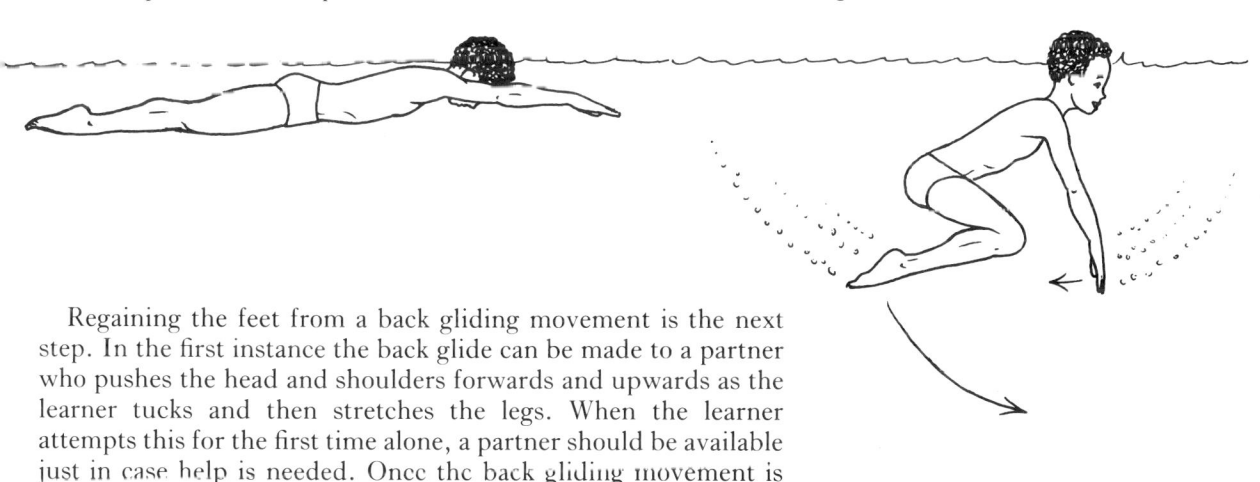

Fig. 3.16

34 First steps – make it enjoyable

As the control of the body in water improves, the learners can be encouraged to try out some variations in regaining the feet.

Can you:
- push off on the front with a float, release the float and then stand up?
- push off on the back with a float, release the float and then stand up?
- regain your feet from a front gliding movement after being towed and then released by a partner?
- regain your feet from a back gliding movement after being towed and then released by a partner?
- push off on your front, roll on to your back and then stand up?
- push off on your back, roll on to your front and then stand up?

Getting the head under the water

By now the learners will be used to getting the face wet and they can start trying to get the head under the water.

Can you:
- get your head completely under the water (partner could check this)?
- see your partner's feet when you go under?
- get your head under and blow bubbles?
- climb through a hoop held vertically beneath the surface?
- pick up an object from the bottom of the pool?
- go under the water with your partner?
- glide, regain your feet and then go under the water?

Some learners will want to hold the pool side or a partner's hand to start with, whereas others will attempt the movement without support. In all cases tell the learners to take one breath only before going under, and to stay under for a few seconds only.

Even at this stage you will find that some learners are still reticent about getting their heads under the water. If there are learners in this category, do not force them into these practices; it must be remembered that certain strokes can be performed without placing the face beneath the surface!

Let's move

The learners have acquired many skills in these early stages, and these can now be organised in an enjoyable way to check progress.

Gliding

Can you:
- glide further on your back or on your front?
- glide further on your front with your head up or with your head down?

- glide further on your back with your head up or with your head back in the water?
- glide further on your back or on your front with your legs together or with your legs apart?
- glide further on your back or on your front with your toes pointing backwards or downwards?
- swim further with alternating or simultaneous leg actions?
- swim further with alternating or simultaneous arm actions?

General

Can you:
- swim far wearing a supportive aid?
- go further on your back or front when wearing a supportive aid?
- jump in, swim a few strokes and stand up?
- hold a float and move by kicking only?
- kick your legs continually for ten seconds when being towed by a partner (Fig. 3.17)?
- jump in, swim a few strokes, stand up and then pick up an object from the bottom of the pool?
- hold a mushroom float for five seconds?

Fig. 3.17

Children who are too small to get their feet on the bottom of the pool will have to practise with supportive aids. Arm and leg actions are still possible and gliding can be done by pushing off entirely from the wall. Although the face can be placed in the water the 'going under' practices cannot be attempted with buoyant support. When these children try to swim unaided, they will need to push off from the steps with an adult helper in close attendance.

Progress will vary according to the individual but they are ready to start learning specific strokes once they can:

- glide;
- regain their feet from front and back gliding movements;
- react with control when water splashes in the face;
- move short distances without a supportive aid.

4 Stroke development – keep it simple

General notes

Columns

The material for each stroke is placed in three columns. These columns are headed:

1. development;
2. practices;
3. progress report.

The development column indicates how the stroke can be learned, and the practice column gives ways of achieving the skills. Under progress report check points are made and questions asked to help the evaluation process.

Demonstrations

Wherever possible a demonstration of the correct movement by a good swimmer or a simple land demonstration by a teacher can help the learner's progress.

Land practices

If the correct movement is going to be achieved it will have to be in the water. However, a 'feel' of the movement out of the water can sometimes be beneficial, e.g. sitting on the side of the pool and practising the life saving or back crawl kick.

Breathing

In general, swimmers tend to breathe in and out through the mouth, but there are times when a nose exhalation may be necessary, e.g. in back crawl swimming and in the tumble turn, water tends to enter the nose and will need clearing.

Arm practices

Pulling practices come later in the learning process, as the near-horizontal position is better achieved by working on kicking and

Back crawl

full stroke activities. As the stroke improves and the arms become stronger, pulling practices can be done much more effectively.

Individuals will develop at their own rate and, in general, it is better that comparisons are not made with others.

Back crawl

Body position (Fig. 4.1)

body:	near-horizontal
head:	slightly raised
hips:	just below the water surface

Fig. 4.1

Fig. 4.2

Legs (Fig. 4.2)

general:	continuous alternating kick
	initiate from the hips
	legs close together
	knees beneath the water surface
downwards kick:	down straight and bend near the bottom of the kick
upwards kick:	straighten at the knee
	toes stretched
	foot turned slightly inwards

Fig. 4.3

Arms

general:	continuous alternating action
entry (Fig. 4.3):	near the shoulder line
	palm facing outwards
pull:	shallow and sideways movement
(beginners)	arms straight
pull (Fig. 4.4):	bend and straighten the arm
(advanced swimmers)	('S' movement)
recovery (Fig. 4.5):	lift the arm
	arm straight
	palm facing outwards

Breathing

once every arm cycle
mainly through the mouth

Fig. 4.4. (a)

Fig. 4.4. (b)

Fig. 4.5

Back crawl 39

Timing (Fig. 4.6)   6 beats to every arm cycle   Fig. 4.6
one arm pulls as the other recovers

Teaching

Once the swimmers are confident in regaining their feet from a back lying position in the water, the stroke can be taught safely. The leg kick should be established early on, and leg and full stroke activities should be practised regularly. As the swimmers become stronger and find that they can perform a continuous arm movement, pulling practices can be added. As the leg kick in back crawl is similar to that of front crawl the two strokes can be developed simultaneously.

Development	Practices	Progress report
1. Regain feet from a supine position	Push away from the side of the pool, glide with the hands by the side and then regain the feet *Variations*: a. Push to a partner who helps with regaining the standing position b. Push away holding a float flat and above the hips	*Can you*: regain your feet without help? regain your feet quickly and effectively?

40 Stroke development – keep it simple

Development	Practices	Progress report
2. Glide and kick	Push away from the pool side, glide with the hands by the sides and then kick vigorously *Variations*: a. Practise gliding and kicking while a partner supports under the armpits and pulls (Fig. 4.7) b. Push away holding a float flat and above the hips and then kick	*Can you*: keep your hips close to the water surface? keep your legs going continuously?

Fig. 4.7

Development	Practices	Progress report
3. Leg-action	Practise kicking over various distances *Variations*: a. Scull with the hands close to the hips (Fig. 4.8) b. Place the hands on the thighs c. Extend the arms beyond the head and hold a float d. Extend the arms beyond the head e. Fins may be worn as long as their use is controlled f. Practise kicking in the front crawl position	Check that a near-horizontal body position and a vigorous and continuous leg movement are maintained by swimming a distance that is appropriate to ability

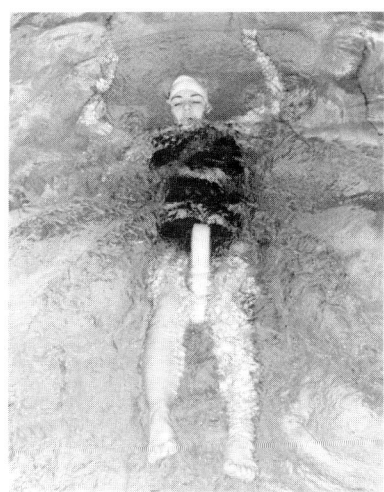

Back crawl 41

Fig. 4.8

Fig. 4.9

Development	Practices	Progress report
4. Glide, kick and pull	Push away from the pool side, glide, kick vigorously and then pull	*Can you*: keep your hips close to the water surface?
5. Arm action	1. Practise arm action standing in the water 2. Practise full stroke over various distances *Variation*: Use fins so that the body position is maintained more easily 3. Practise pulling over various distances (float or pull – buoy between the upper legs) *Variations*: a. Practise pulling with both arms simultaneously (Fig. 4.9) b. Practise pulling with one arm c. Practise with hand paddles	*Can you*: keep the arms moving continuously? enter the arms close to the shoulder line? Encourage a shallow straight arm pull in these early development stages. The pull and push down the body with a bending and straightening at the elbow can come later
6. a. Arm action and breathing	Practise pulling and breathing	*Can you*: breathe regularly? breathe in and out through the mouth?
b. Full stroke and breathing	Practise the full stroke with correct breathing	clear the nose with nasal exhalation?

Development	Practices	Progress report
7. Co-ordination	Practise the full stroke over various distances and at different speeds (Fig.4.10)	*Can you*: kick the legs continuously? pull and recover without stopping? Check that the near-horizontal body position is maintained

Fig. 4.10

Front crawl

Body position (Fig. 4.11)
    body: almost horizontal
    head: slightly raised
           look downwards and forwards
    hips: close to the water surface

Legs (Fig. 4.12)
    general: continuous alternating kick
           initiate from the hips
            legs close together
    downwards kick: straighten at the knee
            toes stretched
            foot slightly inwards
    upwards kick: up straight and bend near the top of the kick

Front crawl 43

Fig. 4.11 ▲ and Fig. 4.12

Fig. 4.13

Arms

general: continuous alternating action
entry (Fig. 4.13):   between the shoulder and the
                               centre line
                         through the fingertips

44 Stroke development – keep it simple

Fig 4.14. (a)
Fig. 4.14. (c)

Fig. 4.14. (b)
Fig. 4.14. (d)

pull (Fig. 4.14):	bend and straighten the arm elbow up
recovery (Fig. 4.15):	lift and bend the elbow and lead the entry with the hand
Breathing (Fig. 4.16)	once every arm cycle turn to the side of the recovery arm mainly through the mouth

Front crawl 45

Fig. 4.15. (a) ← Fig. 4.15. (b)

Fig. 4.16

46 Stroke development – keep it simple

Fig. 4.17

Timing (Fig. 4.17) 6 beats to every arm cycle (there are other variations)
one arm pulls as the other recovers

Teaching

In the early stages, practise the full stroke and leg activities regularly. Once the swimmer is travelling far enough to need a breath, introduce arm and breathing practices in the shallow water (i.e. standing and walking). Continue with full stroke and leg practices but encourage some breathing when performing the full stroke. As the breathing becomes more proficient, longer distances can be swum and arm practices can be added. As the correct breathing movement is essential for maintaining a good body position, it may be necessary to keep checking the technique and going back to the standing and walking practices.

Development	Practices	Progress report
1. Regain feet from a prone position	Push away from the side of the pool, glide with the arms extended beyond the head and then regain the feet *Variations:* a. Push to a partner who helps with regaining the standing position b. Push away holding a float flat on the water surface and keeping the arms extended	*Can you:* regain your feet without help? regain your feet quickly and effectively?

Front crawl 47

Development	Practices	Progress report
2. Glide and kick	Push away from the pool side holding a float, glide and then kick vigorously *Variations:* a. Holding a float, glide and kick to the pool side b. Glide with extended arms towards a partner and kick as the partner pulls	Breathing technique is at the discretion of the swimmer
3. Leg action	Practise kicking *Variations:* a. Hold on to the pool side b. Hold a float and kick over various distances c. With or without a float, kick while in the supine position d. Use a float as resistance (Fig. 4.18) e. Kick with the arms extended beyond the head or down by the sides f. Use fins	*Can you:* keep the legs up? keep the legs going continuously? Check that the leg kick is shallow and vigorous

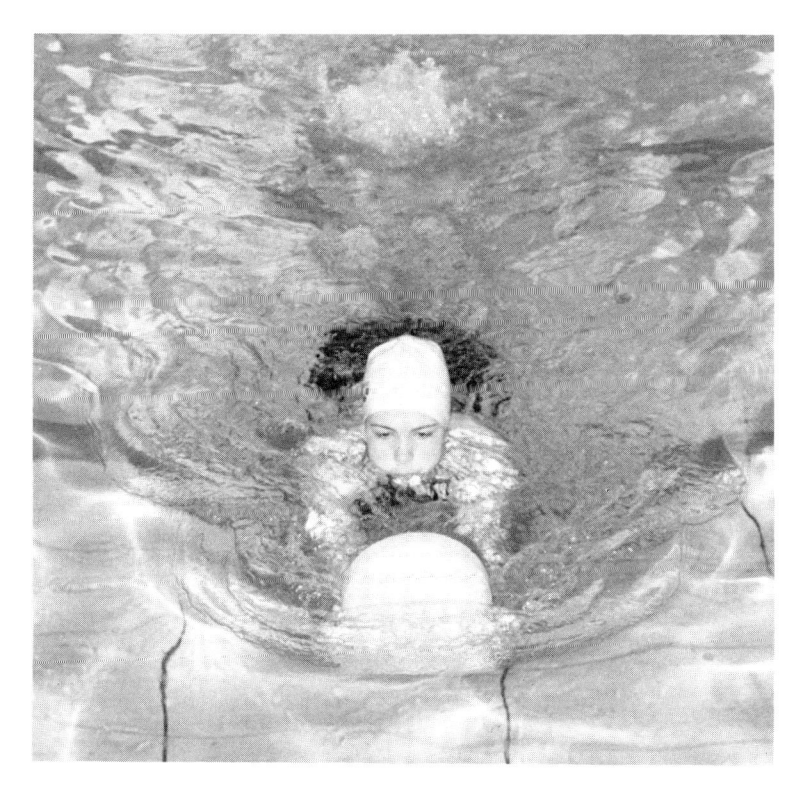

Fig. 4.18

Development	Practices	Progress report
4. Glide, kick and pull	Push away from the pool side, glide with the arms extended beyond the head, kick and pull simultaneously	Practise this movement over short distances. Breathing technique is at the discretion of the swimmer
5. **a.** Glide and breathe	Push away from the pool side, glide with the arms extended beyond the head and breathe out	Check for bubbles under water
b. Arm action and breathing	Standing in a bent position, practise the arm action and breathing *Variations:* **a.** Practise the breathing movement with the breathing side arm only **b.** Practise the arm action and breathing while walking	Make sure that the air has been blown out before inhaling *Can you:* get a good breath? breathe on both sides?
c. Full stroke and breathing	Practise swimming short distances and breathe when the need arises	Check that the swimmer is getting rid of the air
6. Arm action	1. Practise pulling over various distances (float or pull-buoy between the upper legs) (Fig. 4.19) *Variations:* **a.** Practise pulling with one arm **b.** Practise a catch-up stroke (the pulling arm starts only when the recovery arm is placed next to it) **c.** Practise with hand paddles 2. Practise the full stroke but concentrate upon the arms *Variation:* Full stroke with fins on the feet	Breathing technique is at the discretion of the swimmer *Can you:* keep the arms moving continuously? pull beneath the body?
7. Arm action and breathing	Practise the arm action with a regular breathing rhythm	Check that the head is being turned smoothly
8. Co-ordination	Practise the full stroke over various distances and at different speeds	*Can you:* kick the legs continuously? pull and recover without stopping? breathe regularly? Check that the swimmer is looking forwards and downwards Check that the swimmer is developing a rhythmic action

Fig. 4.19

Fig. 4.20

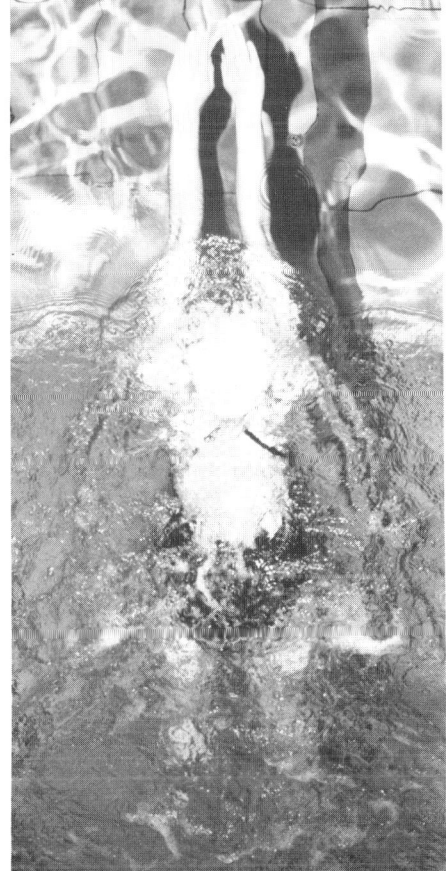

Breast stroke

Body position (Fig. 4.20)

    body: near-horizontal
    head: raised for breathing, lowered as
                                  arms extend
    hips: below the water surface

50 Stroke development – keep it simple

Fig. 4.21. (a)

Fig. 4.21. (b)

Fig. 4.21. (c)

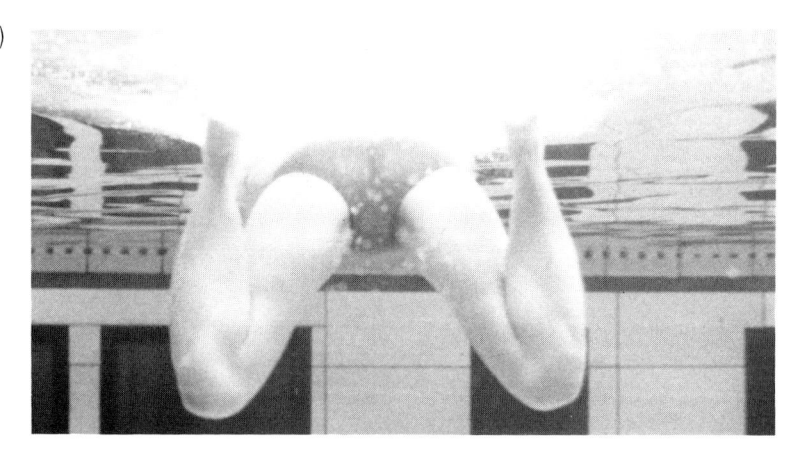

Legs (Fig.4.21)

recovery: bend at the knees and bring the heels up to the buttocks
hook and turn the feet outwards just prior to the kick

kick (Fig. 4.22): drive the legs round and together

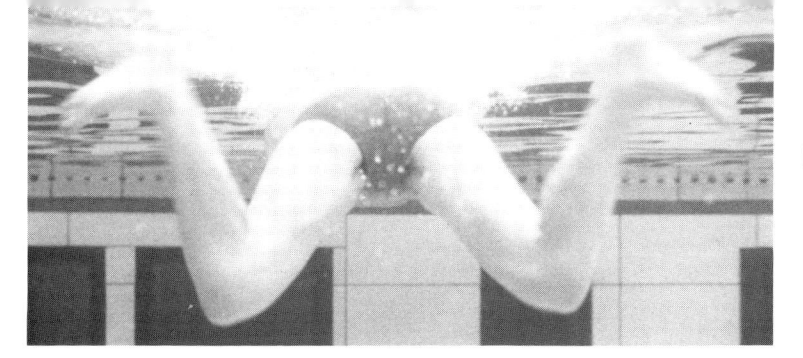

Fig. 4.22. (a)

Fig. 4.22. (b)

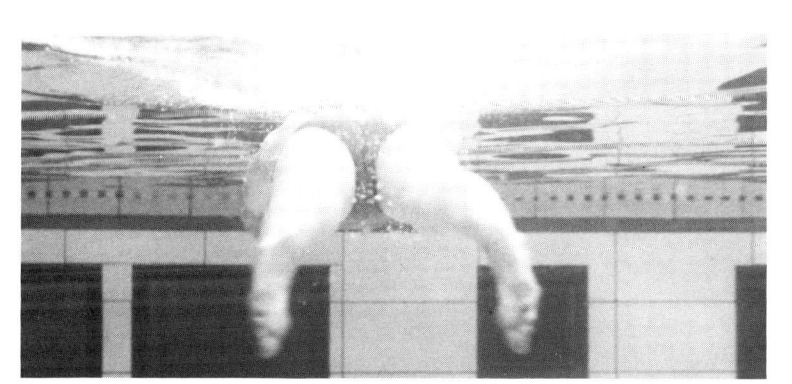

Fig. 4.22. (c)

Fig. 4.22. (d)

Fig. 4.22. (e)

52 Stroke development – keep it simple

Fig. 4.23. (a)

Fig. 4.23. (b)

Fig. 4.23. (c)

Arms

pull: (beginners)	sideways, downwards and backwards
	arms straight
	hands stay in front of a line dropped from the shoulders
pull (Fig. 4.23): (advanced swimmers)	start straight and then bend elbows up
	hands stay in front of a line dropped from the shoulders
recovery (Fig. 4.24):	bring hands inwards and then forwards in a continuous movement

Fig. 4.24 (a)  Fig. 4.24. (b)

Breathing (Fig. 4.25)

Timing
once every arm cycle
to the front at the start of the pull (beginners)
to the front at the start of the recovery (advanced swimmers)
pull, recover arms and legs, kick and stretch (beginners)
arms almost straight before the kick (advanced swimmers) (Fig. 4.26)

Note: for competitive swimmers, some part of the head must break the water surface during each complete cycle of one arm stroke and one leg kick.

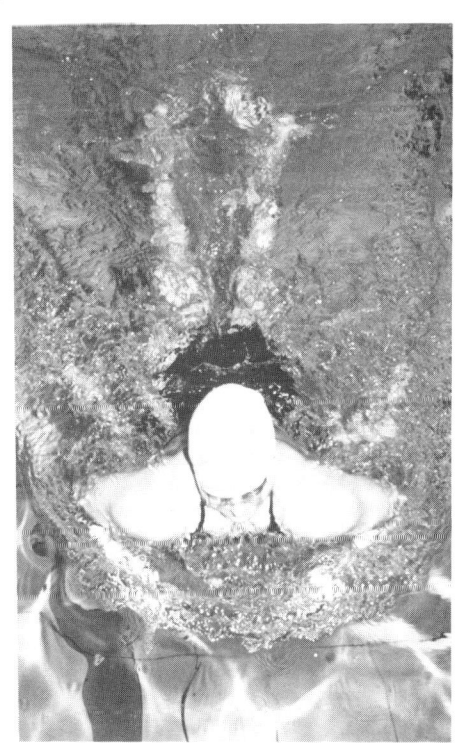

Fig. 4.25

Fig. 4.26.

54 Stroke development – keep it simple

Teaching

In the early stages, practise regaining the feet from a prone glide and attempt the full stroke. Once the swimmers have some idea of the stroke, establish an efficient leg action. The breathing can then be developed through full stroke and arm practices and, as the arm and leg actions become more effective, the timing of the stroke can be improved.

Development	Practices	Progress report
1. Regain feet from a prone position	Push away from the side of the pool, glide with the arms extended beyond the head and then regain the feet *Variations:* a. Push to a partner who helps with regaining the standing position b. Push away holding a float flat on the water surface and keeping the arms extended	*Can you:* regain your feet without help? regain your feet quickly and effectively?
2. Glide and full stroke	Push away from the pool side, glide, pull and kick, stand up *Variations:* a. Push and glide from a crouch position in the water, pull and kick, stand up b. Continue the sequence across the width of the pool c. Try two or three full strokes after the initial glide	Check that the near-horizontal position is obtained before the pull and kick is made *Can you:* get the arms nearly straight before you kick? glide after the kick? Check that the legs are kept close to the water surface
3. Glide and kick	Push away from the pool side holding a float with the arms extended, glide, kick once and then stand up *Variations:* a. Push and glide from a crouch position in the water, kick once and then stand up b. Continue the sequence across the width of the pool (with float) c. Try three or four leg kicks (with float) d. Push away from the pool side and glide in a supine position, holding the float flat on the water surface and above the hips, kick once and then stand up e. Try three or four leg kicks in the supine position (Fig. 4.27)	*Can you:* keep the speed up? keep the legs near the water surface? *Can you:* keep your chin close to the water surface? Check that one kick is completed before the next leg kick starts

Breast stroke 55

Fig. 4.27

Development	Practices	Progress report
4. Leg action	1. Kick widths of the pool in prone and supine positions (with float) *Variations:* a. Try kicking widths of the pool in prone and supine positions with arms placed by the sides or beyond the head b. Use floats as resistance	Ensure that the legs are brought close to the water surface after each kick
Early practice for correcting technique	2. Holding the sides of the pool practise the leg kick (a partner can sometimes guide the legs through the correct movement) *Variations:* a. Swimmer practises the leg action while being pulled across the pool by a partner b. Swimmer can be towed in the supine position	*Can you:* keep the hips up? keep your chin on the water surface? Check that the partner stays low in the water and keeps the swimmer in a near-horizontal position

56 Stroke development – keep it simple

Development	Practices	Progress report
5. a. Full stroke and breathing	Practise the full stroke over short distances concentrating upon the breathing	*Can you:* blow out hard as the arms go forwards? take in a full breath?
b. Arm action and breathing	Practise the arm action and breathing while standing or walking in the shallow end (Fig. 4.28) *Variation:* Practise the arm action and breathing with a float or pull buoy between the upper legs	Check that the breathing rhythm fits in with the stroke action

Fig. 4.28

Development	Practices	Progress report
6. Arm action	Practise the arm action with a float or pull-buoy between the upper legs *Variations:* a. Practise the arm action while kicking with a dolphin movement b. Practise the arm action while trailing the legs c. Practise the arm action and breathe once every two arm cycles	*Can you:* keep your hands in sight even though you are looking forwards? *Can you:* keep the hands beneath the water surface? Check that the swimmer moves from the end of the pull to the recovery with a minimal delay

Life saving kick

Development	Practices	Progress report
7. Co-ordination	Practise various distances using a regular breathing rhythm	Look for a rhythmic stroke
	Variations: a. Try the full stroke with a continuous arm movement b. Try the full stroke with a glide at the end of the recovery c. Try both the straight arm pull and the increasingly bent arm action d. Try delaying the inhalation until the recovery starts	Check that the swimmer is pushing the chin forwards to breathe and that the near-horizontal body position does not alter greatly

Life saving kick

Body position

body: slightly angled
head: slightly raised (to observe subject)
hips: below the water surface (to allow for an effective leg kick beneath the subject)

Legs

recovery (Fig. 4.29): bend at the knees and drop the heels downwards and backwards towards the buttocks
knees slightly spread and beneath the water surface
hook and turn the feet outwards just prior to the kick

kick (Fig. 4.30): drive the legs round and together and straighten

Fig. 4.29

Breathing

once every leg cycle

Teaching

In the early stages practise the leg kick while holding a float flat and above the hips. As the leg kick improves, dispense with the float and either scull with the hands close to the hips or fold the arms across the chest. As this leg kick is used for life saving tows, practices with a partner should be included in the learning process.

The life saving kick should always be taught in conjunction with the breast stroke.

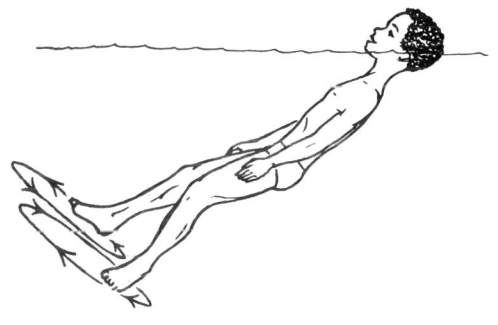

Fig. 4.30

58 Stroke development – keep it simple

Development	Practices	Progress report
1. Regain feet from a supine position	Push away from the side of the pool, glide with the hands by the side and then regain the feet *Variations:* a. Push to a partner who helps with regaining the standing position b. Push away holding a float flat and above the hips	*Can you:* regain your feet without help? regain your feet quickly and effectively?
2. Glide and kick	Push away from the pool side, glide with the hands by the sides and then kick three or four times *Variations:* a. Practise gliding and kicking while a partner supports under the armpits and pulls b. Push away holding a float flat and above the hips and then kick	Check that the head is slightly raised
3. Leg action	Practise kicking over various distances *Variations:* a. Scull with the hands close to the hips (Fig. 4.31) b. Place the hands on the thighs c. Fold the arms across the chest d. Place one hand across the chest and scull with the other e. Try an alternating leg action (egg beater)	*Can you:* keep the knees under the water surface? keep a fast circular foot action going?

Fig. 4.31

Elementary back stroke

Development	Practices	Progress report
4. Kick and breathing	Practise kicking over various distances with a regular breathing rhythm	
5. Towing practice	Practise towing a partner over various distances (Fig. 4.32) *Variations:* a. Subject places a float or pull-buoy between the upper legs b. Subject kicks gently using a back crawl action c. Subject gives no help d. Tow different subjects	Ensure that the subject's face stays above the water surface Check that the tower and subject move as one

Fig. 4.32

Elementary back stroke

Body position

    body: near-horizontal
    head: slightly raised
    hips: below the water surface (to allow for an effective leg kick beneath the water surface)

60 Stroke development – keep it simple

Fig. 4.33

Fig. 4.34

Fig. 4.35

Fig. 4.36. (a)   Fig. 4.36. (b)

Legs

recovery (Fig. 4.33): bend at the knees and drop the heels downwards and backwards towards the buttocks
knees spread with the feet close together
hook and turn the feet outwards just prior to the kick

kick (Fig. 4.34): drive the legs round and together and straighten

Arms

pull (Fig. 4.35): shallow, sideways movement with straight arms to the sides of the body

recovery (Fig. 4.36): bring the bent arms upwards along the body and stretch to a 'Y' position beyond the head
keep below the water surface

Breathing

every arm cycle
inhale during the arm recovery and exhale during the pull

Timing

recover the arms and legs together
kick and pull together
glide

Teaching

Once the swimmers have gained confidence in regaining their feet from a back lying position, practise kicking over various distances. The arm action can then be developed through arm and full stroke practices. As the swimmers become more proficient, work the breathing rhythm into the arm and full stroke movement, and then spend time working on the correct arm and leg co-ordination.

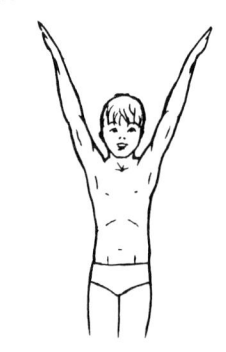

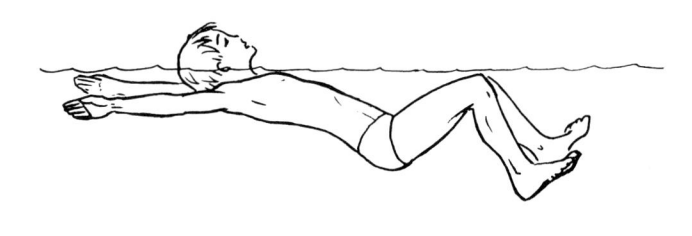

Elementary back stroke 61

Development	Practices	Progress report
1. Regain feet from a supine position	Push away from the side of the pool, glide with the hands by the side and then regain the feet *Variations:* a. Push to a partner who helps with regaining the standing position b. Push away holding a float flat and above the hips	*Can you:* regain your feet without help? regain your feet quickly and effectively?
2. Glide, scull with the hands and kick	Push away from the pool side, glide with the hands by the sides, scull continuously and kick two or three times *Variations:* a. Partner supports under the armpits and pulls b. Push away holding a float flat and above the hips c. Repeat the sequence of glide, scull and kick two or three times and regain the feet going across the width	Check that a near horizontal body position is maintained *Can you:* keep your hips close to the water surface? keep a continuous sculling action going?
3. Leg action	Practise kicking over various distances *Variations:* a. Hold a float flat above the hips b. Hold a float under each arm (Fig. 4.37) c. Place the hands on the thighs d. Practise kicking in the prone position	Check that the kick is a circular and continuous movement *Can you:* get your legs close to the water surface at the end of each kick? feel your feet turning outwards before the kick?

Fig. 4.37

62 Stroke development – keep it simple

Development	Practices	Progress report
4. Arm action	1. Practise the arm action standing in the water 2. Place a float or pull-buoy between the upper legs and gently go through the arm action	Check that the arm action is kept below the water surface
	Varitions: a. Practise pulling over various distances (with float) b. Practise pulling with a back crawl leg action	*Can you:* glide at the end of the pull? feel the surge as you pull?
5.a Arm action and breathing b. Full stroke and breathing	Practise pulling and breathing Practise the full stroke and correct breathing	Check for a regular breathing action
6. Co-ordination	Practise the full stroke over various distances and at different speeds	*Can you:* glide at the end of the pull and kick? glide with your legs close to the water surface?

Fig. 4.38

Butterfly dolphin

Body position (Fig. 4.38)

body:	near-horizontal with some up and down movement
head:	slightly raised look downwards and forwards
hips:	just below the water surface.

Legs (Fig. 4.39)

general:	move the legs simultaneously initiate from the hips
downwards kick:	straighten at the knees toes stretched feet slightly inwards
upwards kick:	up straight and bend near the top of the kick

Butterfly dolphin 63

Fig. 4.39. (a)   Fig. 4.39. (b)

Arms

general (Fig. 4.40): move the arms simultaneously
entry· between the shoulder and the
centre line and through the
fingertips

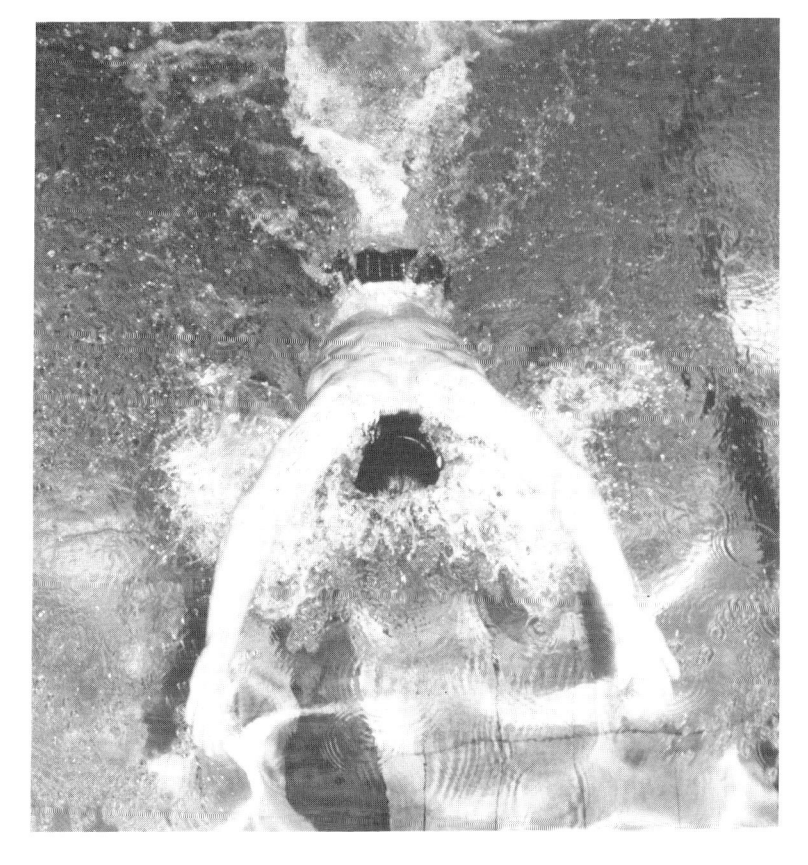

Fig. 4.40

64 Stroke development – keep it simple

Fig. 4.41. (a), (b) and (c)

Fig. 4.42

pull (Fig. 4.41): bend and straighten the arms elbows up
recovery (Fig. 4.42): lift the arms round and low over the water surface

Butterfly dolphin

Breathing once every arm cycle
to the front at the start of the pull (beginners)
to the front at the start of the recovery (advanced swimmers) (Fig. 4.43)

Timing (Fig. 4.44)
general: two leg beats (i.e. two upwards and two downwards movements) to every arm cycle
first downwards kick at the start of the arm pull
second downwards kick at the end of the propulsive arm movement

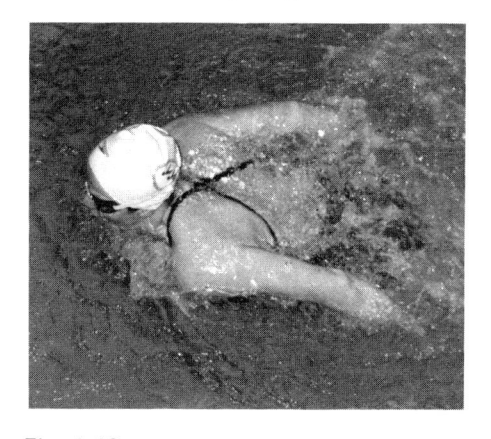

Fig. 4.43

Fig. 4.44. (a), (b) and (c)

Teaching

In the early stages practise the full stroke over short distances with a 'kick followed by arm action' timing, i.e. two or three leg kicks and then an arm action. Work hard at developing a vigorous and shallow leg action and gradually fit into a continuous arm movement. Once the swimmer becomes more proficient and needs to breathe to keep the stroke going, concentrate upon the arm movement and breathing.

The co-ordination of the stroke can be improved by swimming short distances well rather than long distances badly. When performing the full stroke, either concentrate upon kicking continuously with a slow arm action or think about keeping the arms moving and trying to fit a leg kick in. As the stroke becomes more rhythmic and the hips are kept close to the water surface, the breathing movement will become much easier.

66 Stroke development – keep it simple

Development	Practices	Progress report
1. Regain feet from a prone position	Push away from the side of the pool, glide with the arms extended beyond the head and then regain the feet *Variations:* a. Push to a partner who helps with regaining the standing position b. Push away holding a float flat on the water surface and keeping the arms extended	*Can you:* regain your feet without help? regain your feet quickly and effectively?
2. Glide and full stroke	Push away from the pool side, glide, kick two or three times, pull and recover and then stand up *Variations:* a. Continue the sequence across the width of the pool b. Try the kick and pull sequence twice after the initial glide and then stand up.	Encourage the swimmers to complete the leg beats before starting the arm action Check that the face is kept in the water during the stroke sequence *Did you:* have to stand up more than three times? kick with the arms extended beyond the head?
3. Glide and kick	Push away from the pool side holding a float with the arms extended, glide, kick three or four times and then stand up *Variations:* a. Push and glide from a crouch position in the water, kick three or four times and then stand up (with float) b. Continue the sequence across the width (with float) (Fig. 4.45) c. Push away from the pool side and glide in a supine position, holding the float on the water surface and above the hips, kick three or four times and stand up d. Try a sequence of gliding and kicking across the width of the pool e. Try some of these practices without a float in prone, supine and side positions (arms extended beyond the head)	*Can you:* keep the legs close to the water surface? keep a vigorous movement going? There will be some bending at the knees at the top of the upbeat but any emphasis on the bend can distract the swimmer from initiating the movement from the hips The breathing technique can be at the discretion of the swimmer

Butterfly dolphin 67

Fig. 4.45. (a)

Fig. 4.45. (b)

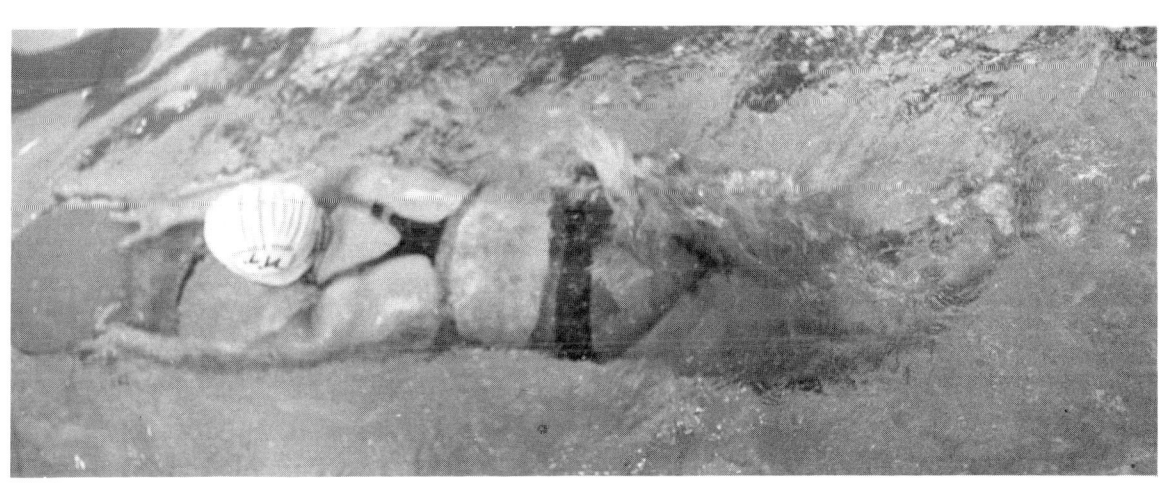

Development	Practices	Progress report
4. Leg action	1. Kick widths of the pool in prone, supine and side positions (with float) *Variations:* a. Try kicking widths of the pool in prone, supine and side positions with arms placed by the sides or beyond the head b. Try kicking short distances in prone, supine and side positions, with arms placed by the sides or beyond the head beneath the water surface c. Use floats as resistance d. Use fins e. Try kicking in a supine position and using a double back crawl arm action	Check that the leg kick is a two-way movement

68 Stroke development – keep it simple

Development	Practices	Progress report
Early practices for correcting techniques	2. Holding the side of the pool, practise the leg kick *Variations:* a. Swimmer practises the leg action while being pulled across the pool by a partner b. Swimmer can be towed in the supine position	Concentrate on kicking upwards from the hips Check that the partner stays low in the water and keeps the swimmer in a near-horizontal position
5.a. Leg and arm actions with breathing	Practise kicking twice, pulling and breathing, recovering the arms and then standing up *Variations:* a. Repeat the sequence across the width of the pool b. Try the sequence two or three times without standing up in between	*Can you:* explode the rest of the air out just before breathing in? keep your chin close to the water surface?
b. Arm action and breathing	Practise the arm action and breathing while standing or walking in the shallow end (Fig. 4.46) *Variation:* Practise the arm action and breathing over a short distance with a float or pull-buoy between the upper legs (allow some leg movement)	Check that the swimmer is not lifting the shoulders to breathe in

Fig. 4.46

Fig. 4.47

Development	Practices	Progress report
6. Arm action	Practise the arm action with a float or pull-buoy between the upper legs over various distances (Fig. 4.47) *Variation:* Try kicking and using one arm only	Breathe every two or three arm cycles so that the swimmer can concentrate upon the arm action *Can you:* keep the arms moving continuously? feel the out and in movement under water?
7. Co-ordination	Practise various distances kicking and pulling simultaneously *Variations:* a. Try kicking and using one arm only b. Concentrate upon a continuous arm action and fit a leg action in c. Concentrate upon a vigorous leg action and fit an arm action in	To give time for two kicks to be made encourage a slow arm action Allow a short glide in the extended arm position in order to allow the second leg kick to be completed. Look for a rhythmic action Check that the hips remain close to the water surface

70 Stroke development – keep it simple

Side stroke

Body position

body:	on the side and near-horizontal
head:	slightly raised and the chin close to the upper shoulder
hips:	below the water surface

Fig. 4.48

Legs

recovery (Fig. 4.48):	spread and bend at the knees and the hips
	move upper leg forwards and lower leg backwards
kick (Fig. 4.49):	vigorously straighten and bring the legs together

Fig. 4.49

Arms

pull and recovery (Fig. 4.50):	pull backwards with the lower arm and recover towards the chin with the upper arm
	push backwards with the upper arm and stretch the lower arm

Fig. 4.50

Breathing

inhale as the lower arm pulls, exhale as the lower arm recovers

Timing

recover the legs as the arms come together
kick as the arms spread (Fig. 4.51)

Butterfly dolphin

Teaching

In the early stages practise regaining the feet from a side glide. Once the swimmers have become familiar with the side position, develop the scissor type leg action and combine with a simplified arm action. The arm action can then be improved and co-ordinated with the breathing rhythm. The final stage is to practise the full stroke over longer distances to establish the correct timing.

Development	Practices	Progress report
1. Regain feet from a side position	Push away from the wall in a side gliding position with arms extended beyond the head and then regain the feet. *Variation:* Push to a partner who helps with the regaining of the standing position	*Can you:* regain your feet without help? move on to your front easily? regain your feet quickly and effectively?
2. Gliding on the side	Practise gliding from the pool side with the bottom arm extended beyond the head and the top arm by the side	*Can you:* balance yourself in the side position? keep the body in a near-horizontal position?
3.a Leg action	Hold the side of the pool and practise the scissor type leg movement (Fig. 4.52) *Variation:* Hold a float in the extended bottom arm and pull with the top arm as the kick is made	Check that the turn is towards the bent arm

Fig. 4.51

72 Stroke development – keep it simple

Development	Practices	Progress report
b. Full stroke	Practise the full stroke over various distances concentrating upon the leg action and just parting the arms as the kick is made *Variation:* Try the movement on the other side	Check that there is a definite recovery and kick *Can you:* recover slowly and scissor vigorously? glide after the kick?
4.**a.** Arm action and breathing	1. Practise the arm action standing and walking sideways 2. Practise the arm action and breathing with a float or pull-buoy between the upper legs	*Can you:* get a good breath in? breathe every arm cycle?
b. Full stroke and breathing	Practise the full stroke concentrating upon the breathing	

Fig. 4.52

Development	Practices	Progress report
5. Co-ordination	Practise the full stroke over various distances *Variations:* **a.** Hold the float in the extended bottom arm and time the push of the top arm with the kick **b.** Place the top arm along the side of the body, and time the pull of the bottom arm with the recovery of the legs **c.** Practise the full stroke and hold a long glide at the end of the kick **d.** Practise towing a partner using an extended arm tow	Check that there is a surge forwards as the kick is made *Can you:* perform the stroke on both the left and right sides? keep going for long distances? keep your partner's face above the water all the time?

Elementary diving – make it safe

5

Early practices

Practices in chest depth water

In the early stages practise submerging in shallow water and opening the eyes.

Can you:
- see the legs of a partner?
- touch a marking on the bottom of the pool?
- pick up an object from the bottom of the pool?
- come to the water surface through a floating hoop?

The next stage is to establish a good glide position as this is important for a safe entry. Practise pushing from the side of the pool and stretching from fingertips to toes. The subject must ensure that the arms enclose and remain above the head.

Can you:
- glide along the water surface?
- glide to the bottom of the pool, tuck the legs and stand up?
- glide to the bottom of the pool, gently arch the body and break the water surface with the hands?
- glide through a partner's legs?
- glide through a hoop held vertically below the water surface?
- glide and move into an armstand?

Early practices from the pool side

Although the depth of water for pool side entries could vary according to the size of the subjects and the type of movement, it is far safer to practise in deep water (3 to 3.5 metres).

To get used to going into the water from the pool side practise gripping the toes over the edge of the pool and jumping in.

74 Elementary diving – make it safe

Can you:
- jump in with your arms stretched above the head?
- stretch from the fingertips to the toes?
- jump in with your arms stretched down by the sides?
- surface by just kicking and holding the arms straight above the head?
- see the water surface as you come up?

As confidence grows, a head-first entry can be attempted. However, it is important that certain safety aspects are emphasised at this time.

1. Protect the head at all times by extending the arms beyond the head.
2. Keep the head between the arms.
3. Grip the pool side with the toes whenever possible.
4. After submersion glide to the water surface by pointing the fingers to the surface and slightly arching the back.
5. If the bottom of the pool is touched after submersion, push upwards with the hands, tuck and swim to the water surface.

With the sitting dive the subject sits on the pool side with the heels resting on the rail or trough (Fig. 5.1)

Fig. 5.1

Early practices 75

Action sequence

Overbalance – keep the head between arms – stretch for entry – glide – point to the water surface

As confidence grows
A late push to lift the hips.

Can you:
- keep your head between your arms on entry?
- stretch on entry?
- see under the water?
- see the bottom of the pool after submerging?
- see the water surface as you start coming upwards?

A progression from the sitting dive is to enter from a kneeling stance. In this particular dive the head is at a greater distance from the water in the starting position. The subject kneels on the pool side with the knee of one leg in line with the edge and the toes of the other leg gripping round the edge of the pool (Fig. 5.2).

Fig. 5.2

Action sequence

Overbalance – keep the head down between the arms – stretch for entry – point to the water surface

As confidence grows
A late push to lift the hips.

Can you
- keep your head between your arms on entry?
- overbalance, stretch and wait?
- feel the longer time in the air?

76 Elementary diving – make it safe

Fig. 5.3

As the subject gains in confidence the head is held higher in the starting position. In the crouch dives (low crouch and semi-crouch) the subject stands on the pool side with the legs slightly apart and the toes of both feet gripping round the edge of the pool (Fig. 5.3).

Action sequence

Overbalance – keep the head down between the arms – wait – stretch for entry – point to the water surface

As confidence grows

A late push to lift the hips.
With the higher starting position the subject is going to enter with more force and the stretching of the arms cannot be over emphasised. If at any time during these practices the arms bend or give way, go back to the earlier gliding practices.

Can you
- keep your arms straight on entry?
- keep stretched under water?
- control your movement to the surface?

The lunge dive is sometimes used as a progression to a higher starting position. In this dive the subject stands, slightly crouched, on the pool side with the toes of one foot gripping round the edge of the pool and the other foot about half a metre back and a little to one side (Fig. 5.4).

Early practices 77

Fig. 5.4

Fig. 5.5

Action sequence

Overbalance – lift the back leg – keep the head down between the arms – wait – stretch for entry – point to the water surface

Can you:
- bring both legs together?
- bring both legs in line with the body?

The dive that gives the subject a good grounding in vertical entry dives is the spring header. The subject stands in an upright position on the pool side with the legs together and the toes of both feet gripping round the edge of the pool. The arms are extended beyond the head with the fingers pointing outwards and upwards (Y position). The subject bends at the hips and knees and brings the body slightly forwards (Fig. 5.5).

Action sequence

Overbalance – drive the hips upwards – wait – bring the arms together – stretch for entry – glide and point to the water surface

Can you
- drive upwards immediately you overbalance?
- feel your hips going upwards?
- feel yourself stretching on entry?
- keep the splash down to a minimum as you enter?

Plunge dive

With the plunge dive the swimmer enters the water in a near-horizontal position with the body fully extended. It is frequently taught before the vertical entry dives as it is a more obvious follow-up to the gliding practices. In addition, it can be performed safely by the swimmer without fear of turning a somersault under the water and becoming disorientated.

Before attempting the plunge dive the swimmer should enter the water and practise pushing and gliding from the pool side. During this practice the swimmer must stretch from fingertips to toes and squeeze the head between the arms.

In the plunge dive the standing position on the pool side must give stability. The swimmer stands in a semi-crouch position with the legs slightly apart and the toes of both feet gripping round the edge of the pool. The hands are placed together with the palms downwards and the fingers pointing at the water surface approximately two metres away from the pool side.

Action sequence

Overbalance – drive outwards – keep the head down between the arms – tense in flight and on entry – glide – point the fingers to the water surface

As the swimmer gains confidence in performing the dive, the arm position in the basic stance may be changed. The arms are now placed in an extended position just behind the hips with the palms facing backwards and upwards (Fig. 5.6). The swimmer looks forwards and downwards at a point just beyond entry.

Action sequence

Overbalance – swing the arms forwards – drive outwards – keep the head down between the arms – tense in flight and on entry – glide – point the fingers to the water surface

Once the swimmer is performing the plunge dive effectively, other practices may be tried. However, it must be noted that where there are glide variations the adjustments must only be made as the glide speed decreases.

Can you
- plunge dive and glide more than seven metres?
- plunge dive and glide further if you start with your arms behind your hips?
- go further if you plunge dive and glide with your feet cocked?
- go further if you plunge dive and glide with your legs slightly apart?
- plunge dive, glide and then turn onto your back?
- plunge, dive, glide, turn onto your back and then onto your front again?

Fig. 5.6. (a), and (b)

Fig. 5.7

Plain header

Depth of water 3 to 3.5 metres

Basic position (Fig. 5.7)

    toes: grip the pool side
    legs: together
    body: upright and firm
    head: look forwards
    arms: Y position

Can you
- maintain an upright position?
- keep the arms, head, body and legs in line?

Action sequence (Fig. 5.8)

Bend at the knees and bring the trunk slightly forwards – drive the hips upwards – maintain a slight pike in flight – bring the arms together – straighten at the hips – stretch for entry – glide – point the fingers to the water surface

Can you
- drive immediately the body overbalances?
- maintain a slight pike in flight?
- hold the Y position for most of the flight?
- bring the arms together before entry?
- keep the arms locked above the head after submersion?

80 Elementary diving – make it safe

Fig. 5.8

Divers often make adjustments in flight (e.g. increase hip bend) to enter closer to the vertical position. However, rather than make these adjustments, it would be better to go back to the spring header practice and work on the basic stance and take-off positions.

Water safety skills – get involved

Survival

Every year drownings occur in swimming pools, domestic baths, ponds, lakes, reservoirs, rivers, canals and the sea. In many of the incidents drowning would not have resulted if various safety precautions had been taken.

If people would learn to swim competently and not take unnecessary risks near, on or in water, many drownings would be prevented. However, even good swimmers can take chances and put their lives in danger; if they get cramp in deep cold water or try and swim in a fast moving current they may have difficulty getting to safety.

By being able to perform some of the skills needed in emergency situations, some fatalities may be avoided. These skills include:

- entries;
- submerging and swimming underwater;
- treading water;
- floating and drownproofing;
- use of clothing and other aids;
- exits.

Such skills can only be regarded as an introduction to the survival area, as they are usually taught in warm, indoor swimming pools under close supervision. If an indoor survival programme can give swimmers the confidence to act calmly in a swimming emergency, to show respect for water and to discourage risk taking, a start will have been made in understanding the concept of water safety.

Entry

Entry practices should always be carried out in deep water. This way the swimmers can concentrate on the entry skill without fear of hitting the bottom of the pool. Although the bottom may be

82 Water safety skills – get involved

reached with the straight entry, much of the force will have dissipated on the way down.

If the water is known to be deep a safe and simple technique is to enter feet first in an extended position:

- Get a firm grip with the front foot.
- Look straight ahead.
- Step sharply forwards with the back leg.
- Quickly bring the front leg in line with the back leg.

Straight jump

- Press the arms to the sides.
- Stretch the body.
- Point the toes.
- Wait for the entry.
- Sink.
- Push off from the bottom of the pool (use a scissor or breast stroke kick if the bottom is not reached).
- Reach upwards with your hands.

If the entry is made with clothes flapping about the face, place the arms across the chest to hold some of the clothing down (Fig. 6.1).

Jumping into unknown or shallow water requires an entry that prevents the swimmer going too deep. This can be done by using the straddle or tuck techniques.

Both techniques can be started from a run, but it is safer to practise from a standing position in the early stages. When the run is introduced it is important that the surface is not a slippery one and that the run is a controlled two or three paces only.

- Get a firm grip with the front foot.
- Look straight ahead.

Straddle jump

- Bring the back leg sharply forward.
- Drive with the front foot.
- Drive outwards.
- Hold a running position in flight.
- Hold the arms sideways and slightly bent.
- Wait for entry.
- Wait until the water reaches the waist.
- Scissor the legs and push down with the hands (Fig. 6.2)

Tuck jump

- Get a firm grip with the front foot.
- Look straight ahead.
- Step sharply forwards with the back leg and drive with the front foot.
- Drive outwards.
- Quickly bring the front leg in line with the back leg.
- Press the arms to the sides of the body.
- Just prior to entry tuck the knees to the chest (Fig. 6.3).

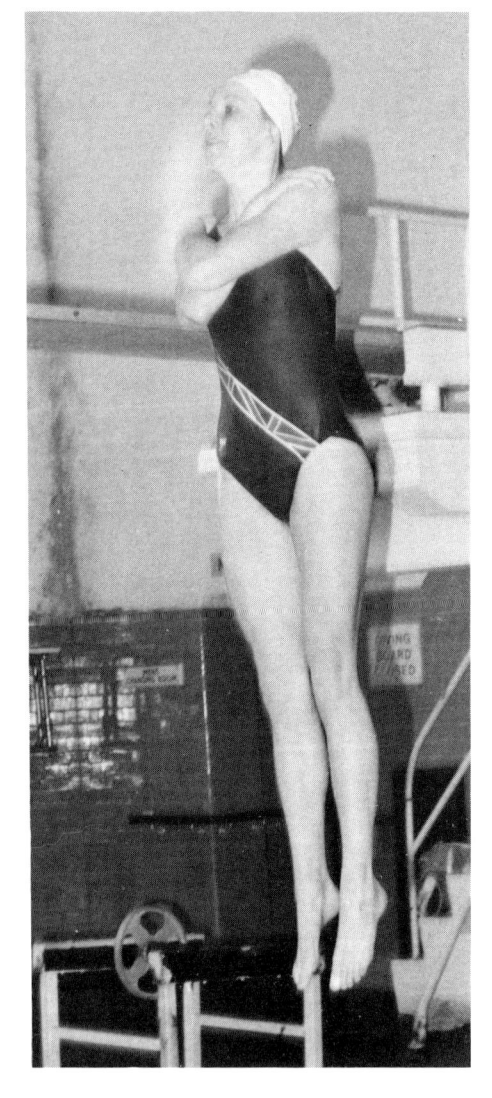

Fig. 6.1

Survival 83

Fig. 6.2

- Hold the front of the legs.
- Wait for entry.
- Wait until the water reaches the waist.
- Kick down with the legs (breast stroke type movement) and push down with the hands.

Once the swimmers can perform these skills correctly and safely they can attempt some variations.

Can you:
- perform a straight jump from the one metre board (Fig. 6.4)?
- perform a straight jump from the three metre board?
- do a straddle jump from the side and keep your head above the water?
- do a tuck jump from the side and keep your head above the water?
- do a straddle jump from the one metre board?
- do a tuck jump from the one metre board?

At this stage do *not* proceed any higher than the one metre board for the tuck and straddle jumps and any higher than the three metre board for the straight jump.

Submerging and swimming underwater

Sometimes it may be necessary to submerge and swim a short distance underwater to avoid obstacles or to rescue somebody from the bottom of the pool. With both the submersion and the swim there are several ways the skills can be carried out, and it is important that the swimmers find their most efficient techniques:

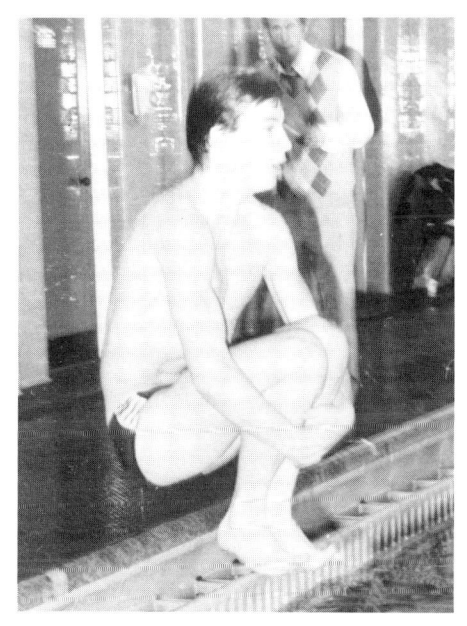

Fig. 6.3
Fig. 6.4

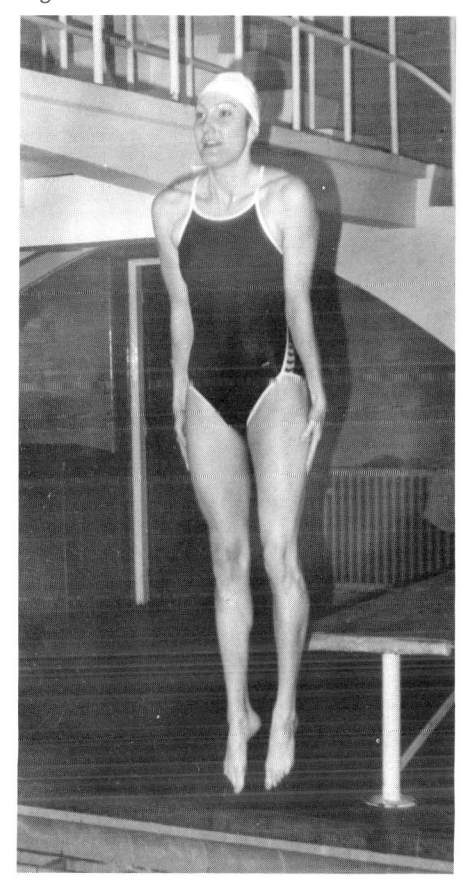

Head first:
- Swim using breast stroke or front crawl.
- Take a deep breath.
- Pull the head down.
- Pike vigorously at the hips.
- Reach down with the arms and straighten the legs in line with the trunk.
- Swim in the required direction once the body has submerged. (Fig. 6.5).

Fig. 6.5. (a)   Fig. 6.5. (b)

Feet first:
- Tread water.
- Kick and push downwards.
- As the body rises place the arms close to the sides and bring the legs together.
- Stretch.
- Sink.
- Tuck and swim in the required direction (Fig. 6.6).

For greater depth the swimmers can either sink and sweep the arms upwards or sink with the arms extended above the head (Fig. 6.7).

Swimming under water
- an alternating arm movement with a crawl kick, i.e. dog's paddle;
- a breast stroke using a long arm pull to the side;
- a breast stroke arm action using a long arm pull with a crawl kick.

Fig. 6.6. (a)

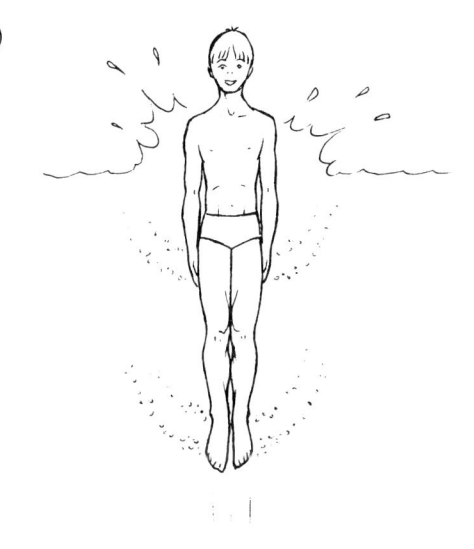

Fig. 6.6. (b)

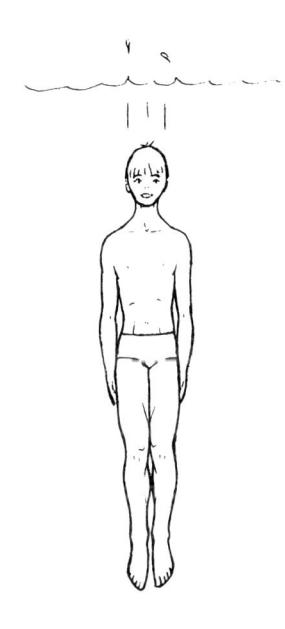

Fig. 6.7

By combining the submerging and underwater swimming skills many interesting practices can be tried.

Can you:
- submerge head first and swim through a hoop?
- submerge feet first, tuck and swim forwards through a hoop?
- submerge and pick up an object from the bottom of the pool?
- submerge and swim five metres under water?
- submerge and swim through a partner's legs?
- jump in from the pool side, swim five metres, submerge and swim five metres under water?

All submerging and underwater practices must be supervised carefully and the swimmers kept to depths no greater than two metres. Even at these depths water exerts pressure on the ears and nose, and it is not sensible to practice these skills with a cold or an ear infection.

Treading water and floating

Treading water and floating can conserve energy by keeping all movements to a minimum.

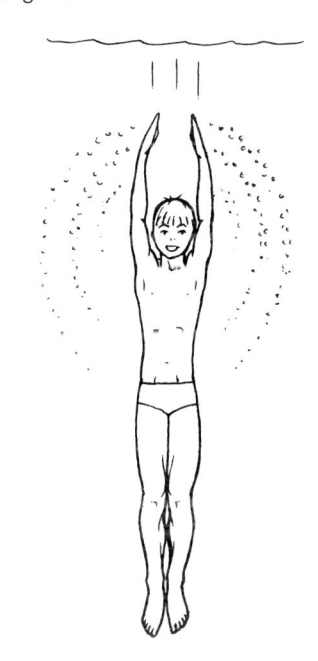

86 Water safety skills – get involved

Treading water (Fig. 6.8)
- Place the head back in the water.
- Control the breathing.
- Scull slowly with the hands.
  Use *either* a modified breast stroke movement;
  or an egg beater;
  or a modified scissor kick.

Fig. 6.8. (a)

Fig. 6.8. (b)

Fig. 6.8. (c)

With the breast stroke kick circle the legs without bringing them together; with the egg beater circle the legs, as in the breast stroke kick, but alternately; with the scissor kick do not complete the movement across. With these leg kicks the body tends to be in a near-vertical position, but, if a bent leg cycling movement is used, it is more efficient to assume a position closer to the horizontal (Fig. 6.9).

Fig. 6.9

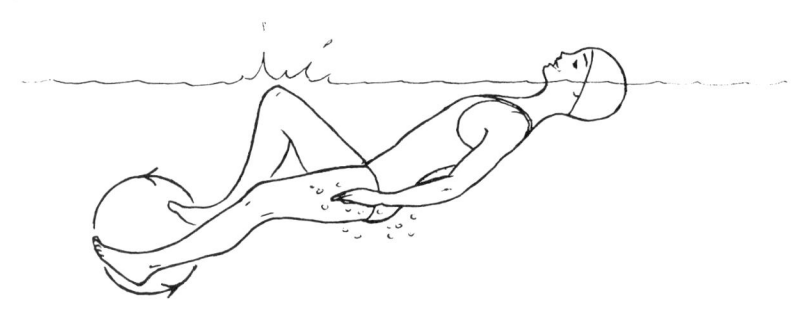

Floating

- Place the head back in the water.
- Keep the hands by the side.
- Control the breathing.

As long as a good supply of air is kept in the lungs and the swimmer waits until the body has adjusted itself in the water, a vertical float can be achieved by most humans.

If swimmers assume a near-vertical position with the face in the water and the arms outstretched beyond the head, a drownproofing technique can be tried. After exhaling beneath the surface, a downward movement of the arms will raise the body and allow for a quick inhalation. The arm movement is not very forceful and should be just enough to get the mouth clear of the water. Once the breath is taken the face is lowered back into the water (Fig. 6.10).

In the learning phase swimmers may find that they can concentrate on the movements and position if they practise wearing a supportive aid (e.g. arm bands). However, once they are performing the skills effectively without an aid the swimmers can try other variations.

Fig. 6.10. (a)

Can you:
- tread water with one hand behind your back?
- tread water with two hands behind your back?
- tread water holding one leg?
- keep afloat by using only the arms?
- do a vertical float?
- float with bent legs?
- do a mushroom float?
- keep afloat using a drownproofing technique?
- float in a horizontal position?
- float for two minutes?
- tread water for five minutes?
- tread water with your hands placed on your head?
- tread water and wave with the arms?
- tread water using different kicks?
- tread water wearing different articles of clothing?
- float wearing different articles of clothing?

Fig. 6.10. (b)

Use of clothing and other aids

Wide-mesh and loosely woven garments do not make good inflatable aids, and should be discarded immediately they become a dangerous hindrance. A woollen jumper does not inflate, and it becomes extremely heavy when it is waterlogged. Such garments as cotton shirts, trousers and dresses can be inflated with ease and used as buoyancy aids.

If clothing is not taken off with care, swimmers can soon get caught up in a garment and find that their limb movements or breathing can be affected. A pair of trousers that is just kicked off can get caught around the legs, and a shirt can get entangled

Fig. 6.10. (c)

around the head if it is dragged off. Where possible, buttons and fasteners should be undone and garments taken off like a coat. If the garment cannot be taken off in this way, try to slip it downwards. Failing this, gather the garment near the shoulders, take a breath and take it over the head in a fast, controlled movement. Trousers should be undone and gathered around the lower legs and then removed with the hands (Fig. 6.11).

Inflation of clothing

Trousers

- Stretch the trousers out.
- Pull the zip up or fasten the buttons.
- Tie a knot low down in each trouser leg.
- Hold the waistband.
- *Either* sweep the trousers through the air from a position close to the head (Fig. 6.12);
  or hold the waistband with one hand just beneath the surface and splash air into the garment with the other hand;
  or plunge air into the trousers by bringing the free hand down vigorously to the garment opening;
  or take the opening beneath the water surface and blow air into the garment.

Once the garment is inflated, the swimmer must seal up the opening and keep the waistband under the water surface. The garment can be placed between the legs or it can be made into a

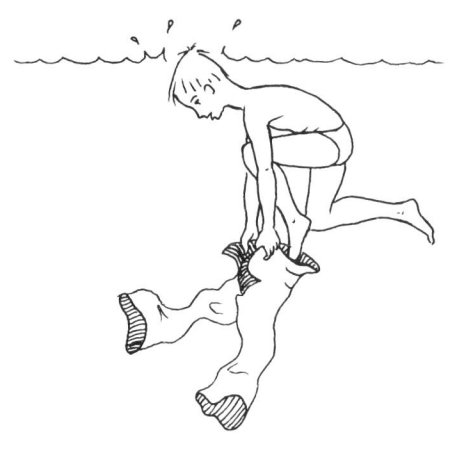

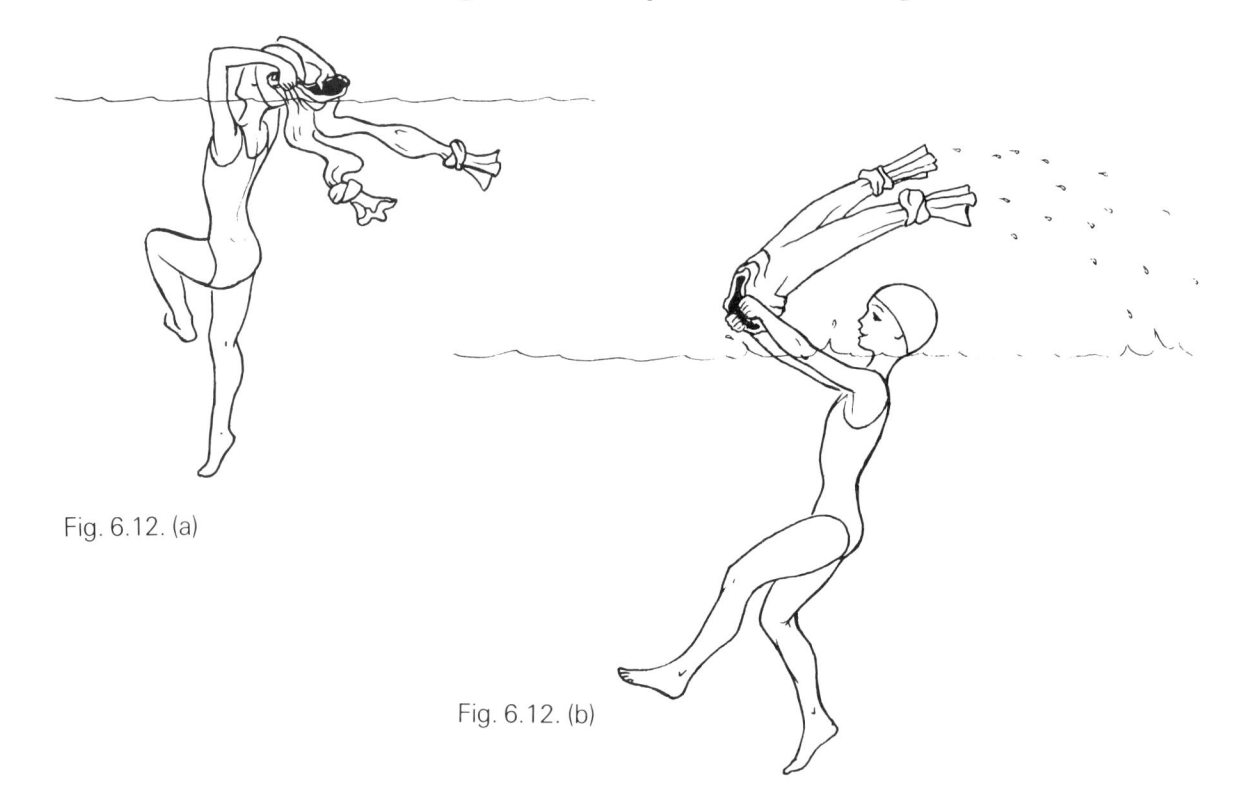

Fig. 6.11

Fig. 6.12. (a)

Fig. 6.12. (b)

Survival 89

life jacket by tying the legs together. Blouses, shirts, dresses and skirts can all be used in a similar way, although skirts can sometimes be more effective if they are kept on. In the early stages, inflation of clothing should be practised in safety in shallow water. Once the swimmer is able to inflate clothing quickly and successfully other practices may be encouraged.

Can you:
- inflate more than four pieces of clothing?
- support yourself in four different ways using one piece of clothing?
- inflate a piece of clothing in three different ways?
- stay afloat for more than five minutes using an inflated garment?
- inflate a garment in less than thirty seconds and then use it as a buoyancy aid?
- remove a garment and inflate it in less than sixty seconds and then use it as a buoyancy aid?
- find a garment that will keep two swimmers afloat?
- swim one hundred metres keeping a garment inflated?

Use of other equipment

Other equipment that can support swimmers in water may also be tried out in a swimming pool. For example, a plastic bottle and a large ball can be effective buoyancy aids. However, it is safer to carry out all the initial practices in shallow water and to progress to deeper water only once the equipment has been found to support the body.

Exits

If the water is at deck level it is relatively simple to climb out on to the side. However, some swimmers have difficulty getting out when the water is below the level of the pool side. In such cases the swimmers need to develop an exit technique:

- Place the hands on the pool side with the arms shoulder width apart.
- Sink down in the water.
- Simultaneously pull and kick with a breast stroke type movement.
- Bring the shoulders over the hands.
- Push or roll out (Fig. 6.13).

Once this technique is perfected the swimmers may try it at speed or as part of a survival sequence:

Can you:
- get out of the pool in less than twenty seconds?
- swim into the side and get out without stopping?
- jump in, swim one hundred metres and then get out of the pool?
- jump in and get out of the pool three times in succession?

Fig. 6.13. (a)

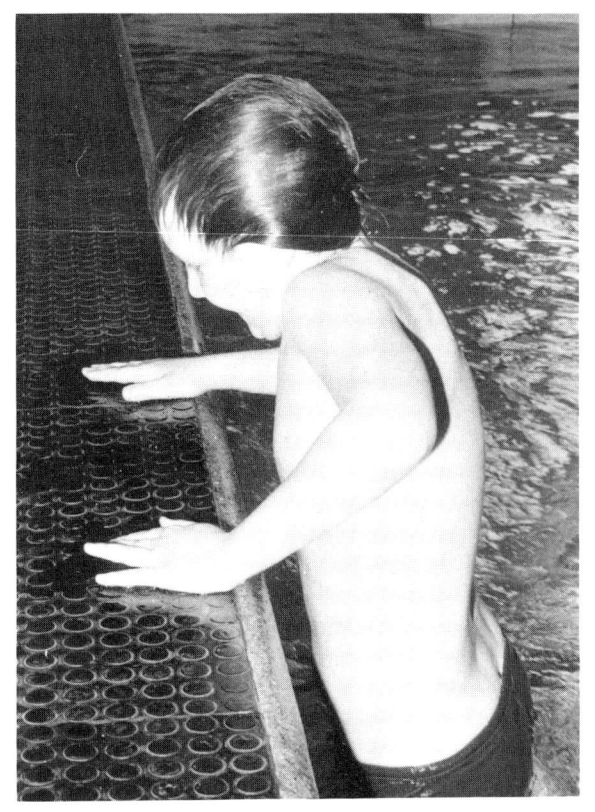

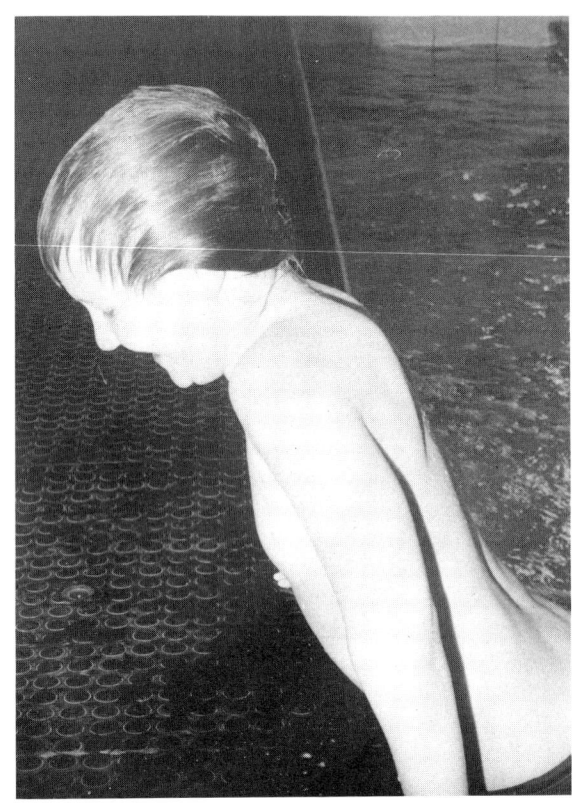

Fig. 6.13. (b)

Cold water

Many drownings take place in open and cold water. As water is twenty times more effective than air in carrying away body heat (by the processes of conduction and convection), survival techniques used in warm water are not always applicable.

In cold water, blood flow in the superficial vessels of the 'shell' (the skin) is quickly switched to the deeper vessels, helping to maintain a 'core' temperature of approximately 37 °C. (The term 'core' denotes the deep central areas of the body and includes the heart, lungs and abdominal organs.) This redistribution of blood helps to minimise heat loss and the skin and fat deposits help to further insulate the body. If the person starts to swim, the blood circulates to bring heat from the core to the peripheral tissues, accelerating the cooling process. In general, children tend to be thinner than adults and lose heat more rapidly.

The trunk is vulnerable to cold as there are parts that have a minimal covering of fat (e.g. sides of the chest) with the blood flow close to the body surface.

To prevent rapid heat loss, clothing should be kept on and only the very heavy garments should be removed. Swimming must be kept to a minimum because this action increases blood flow to the arms and legs, removing heat from the vital organs of the core,

Fig. 6.14

including the brain. A tight, semi-tucked position will be advantageous, helping to conserve body heat (Fig. 6.14).

In conclusion it should be remembered that cold water attacks the body of both the weak and strong swimmer alike, and that swimming competence in a warm indoor pool cannot guarantee safety in open waters.

Life saving

Swimmers and non-swimmers alike can all get into difficulty in water; accidents, water and physical conditions can all dictate the severity of the situation. Some subjects may be able to shout and attract attention, while others may have to fight frantically to keep the head above the water surface. However, in virtually all conscious victims, the facial expression will indicate anything from anxiety to panic. The unconscious victim will usually be limp in the water and can be found anywhere between the bottom and the water surface.

A person hanging on to an air-bed that is drifting out to sea, or a swimmer who is having difficulty getting back to shore are all signs of danger. In general, the person does not appear to be calm or in control of the situation.

Action

Life saving authorities throughout the world tend to favour a particular rescue sequence which entails entering the water only as a last resort. The idea of diving into the water and rescuing a person may appear heroic but it also may be dangerous.

92 Water safety skills – get involved

Sequence

1. If you can reach the casualty?
   - Keep low and slightly away from the edge.
   - Hold on to something secure with one hand or be anchored by a second person (Fig. 6.15).

Fig. 6.15

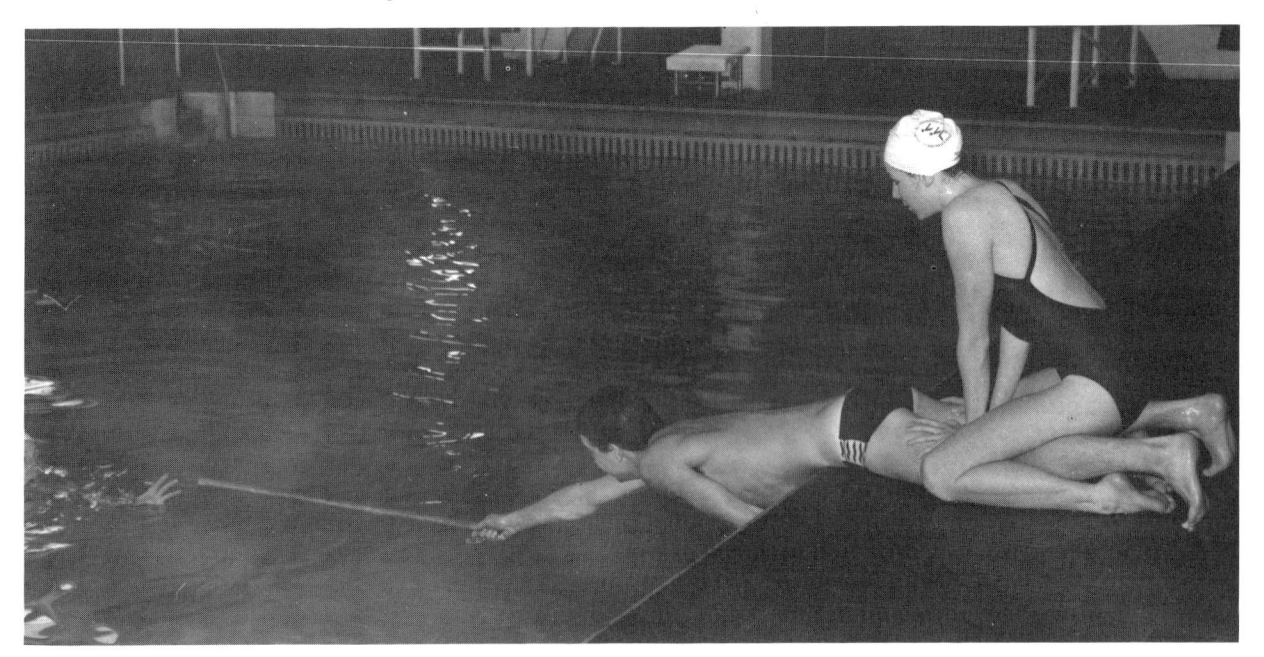

- Extend your reach with an assist (e.g. towel, branch, clothing).
- Pull in, keeping your body weight as far back as possible.

2.a. If you cannot reach throw a floatable object.
   - Stand in a throwing position slightly away from the edge.
   - Use a throwing movement that is familiar to you (i.e. underarm or overarm).
   - Prepare the casualty for the throw.
   - Assess the wind and water conditions.
   - Throw within arm's reach.
   - Encourage the casualty to kick towards the side.

  b. Can you throw a rope, life belt or a floatable object tied to the end of a rope (Fig. 6.16)?
   - Coil the rope.
   - Stand in a throwing position slightly away from the edge.
   - Use an underarm throw unless circumstances dictate something different (i.e. throwing over a fence).
   - Prepare the casualty for the throw.
   - Assess the wind and water conditions.
   - Throw within arm's reach.
   - Bring in the casualty with a controlled pulling action.

Life saving 93

Fig. 6.16
Fig. 6.17

3. If you cannot reach the casualty or throw an object accurately over the required distance, can you *wade* into shallow water and then either reach or throw accurately?
   • Enter feet first and focus on the casualty.
   • Use a stick to prod the bottom for obstructions or deep water.
   • Wade to hip depth.
   • Spread legs for stability.
   • Keep the weight on the back foot.
   • Use the appropriate reaching or throwing rescue (Fig. 6.17)
   • A human chain may sometimes be possible.

4. If the distance is too great for reaching, throwing and wading, are there any boats available?
   • Check that the boat is seaworthy.
   • Check that the boat is properly equipped.
   • Be sure that you can control the boat.
   • Take any additional buoyant aids.
   • Approach the casualty stern first.
   • Either help the casualty over the stern of the boat or help the casualty maintain contact with the boat until help arrives.

94 Water safety skills – get involved

5. If you have to swim towards the casualty, take a buoyant aid with you (e.g. beach ball, large plastic squash container).
   - Enter feet first and focus on the casualty.
   - Swim and prepare the casualty for the rescue as you get within shouting distance.
   - Keep your distance from the casualty as you pass over the buoyant aid.
   - Encourage the casualty to kick towards the side.
   - Swim by the casualty but at a distance that would prevent you being grasped.
   - Use a side stroke or life saving kick.

6. If you have to tow the casualty, can you find a towing aid? (The aid must be long enough to prevent the victim grasping the rescuer.)
   - Enter feet first and focus on the casualty.
   - Swim and prepare the casualty for the rescue as you get within shouting distance.
   - Keep your distance as you pass the aid to the casualty.
   - Instruct the casualty to hold the aid with two hands.
   - Encourage the casualty either to hold the aid in a front position with arms extended and head up or in a back position with the aid held close to the chest.
   - Tow with straight arm.
   - Encourage the casualty to kick gently.
   - Constantly watch the casualty.
   - Use a side stroke or life saving kick.

7. As a last resort, can you tow a casualty effectively using a contact hold?
   - Enter feet first and focus on the casualty.
   - Swim and prepare the casualty for the rescue as you get within shouting distance.
   - Keep a safe distance and approach the casualty from behind

Extended arm chin tow (Fig. 6.18)
   - Take hold of the casualty under the chin and tow with a straight arm.
   - Use a side stroke or life saving kick.

Fig. 6.18

Fig. 6.19

OR Bent arm chin tow (Fig. 6.19)
- Take hold of the casualty's chin with a bent arm and keep your elbows in contact with the shoulder.
- If holding with the right arm keep the casualty's head close to your right shoulder.
- Keep the casualty above you.
- Use a life saving kick.

OR Cross chest tow
- Reach over the casualty's shoulder, across the chest and hold under the far armpit.
- Rest the casualty on your hip.
- Keep the casualty above you.
- Use a side stroke.

General
- Pull with your free arm.
- Watch the casualty carefully.
- Keep the casualty's face above the water surface.
- Encourage the casualty to kick gently.

Some early towing practices

1. Imagine that a float is a casualty: swim widths or lengths keeping the float as steady as possible using bent arm and straight arm tows.
2. Imagine that a float is a casualty: practise changing direction keeping the float as steady as possible.
3. Casualty places a float between the legs: tow the casualty using bent arm and straight arm tows.
4. Casualty places a float between the legs: tow the casualty using the left or right arm as the towing arm.
5. In the shallow end of the pool: one group of pupils makes waves with floats and a second group of pupils swim through the waves keeping floats as steady as possible (Fig. 6.20).

Fig. 6.20

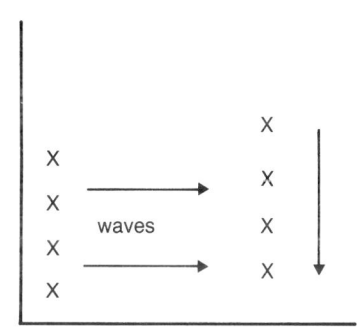

Water safety skills – get involved

6. In the shallow end of the pool: one group of pupils makes waves with floats and a second group of pupils swims through the waves towing (chin hold) casualties who are supported by floats between the legs.
7. Once the pupils become competent at towing supported casualties they can start towing unsupported casualties for short distances.

It is important that the emphasis from the start is on CARE for the casualty. However, this caring attitude can only be achieved if the practice is adjusted to the swimming ability of the pupils. Towing an unsupported victim is a difficult skill, and if a pupil's swimming ability is not at the required standard, the casualty is likely to suffer.

Expired Air Method of Resuscitation (E.A.R.)

Condition of the casualty:
a) no response to the question 'Are you all right?'
b) no apparent chest movement or breathing noises.
c) casualty's ears, lips and nails may appear bluish because of the lack of oxygen in the blood

	Action	Notes
1.	Place the casualty on the back (Fig. 6.21)	Ensure that the casualty's head is well protected as you place it in the back lying position
2.	a. Gently tilt the head backwards and lift the jaw b. Check that the mouth and nose are clear of any obstructions *Response:* a. Casualty may start breathing and gain consciousness b. Casualty may start breathing and remain unconscious c. Casualty may regain consciousness or remain unconscious but may start breathing in a noisy way d. Casualty does not regain consciousness or start breathing	The tilt can be made by gently lifting the neck and pushing on the forehead. This action will open the airway and move the tongue away from the back of the throat. Tell the casualty that all is well and that there is no need to worry Place in the recovery position Check for obstructions in the mouth or nose If the casualty's condition does not change – further action must be taken immediately

Life saving 97

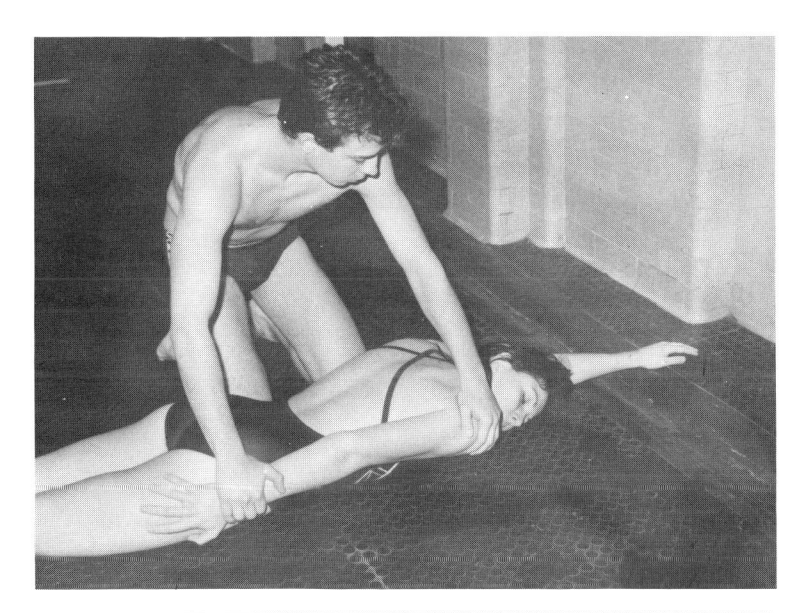

Fig. 6.21. (a)

Fig. 6.21. (b)

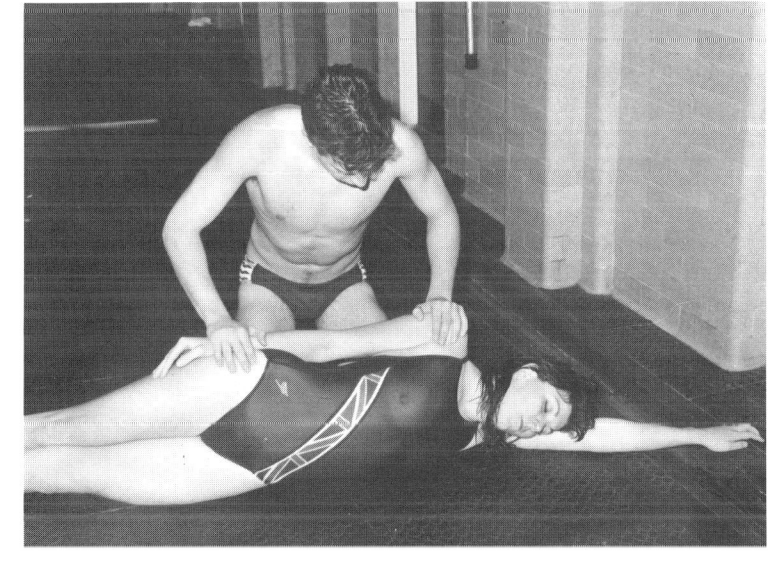

Fig. 6.21. (c)

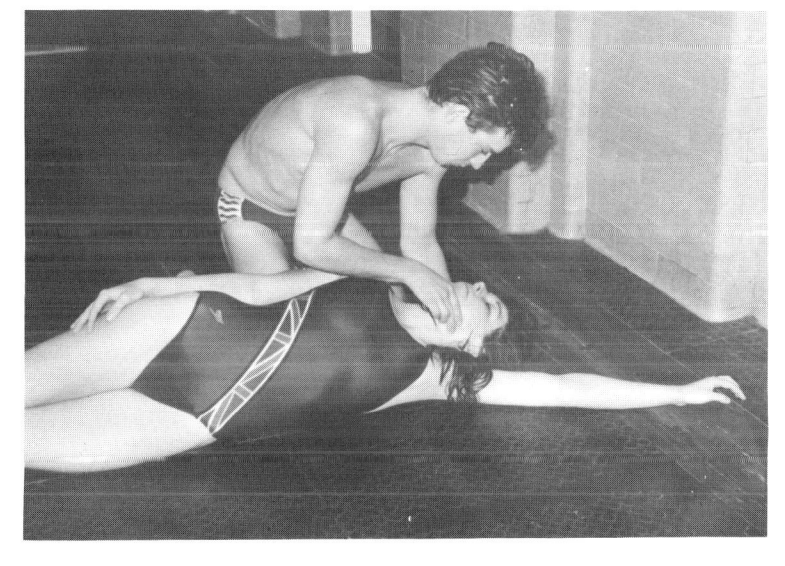

98 Water safety skills – get involved

Action	Notes
3. **a.** *Mouth-to-mouth:* Make an air-tight seal over the victim's mouth with your own Keep the head back and jaw lifted Pinch the casualty's nose (Fig. 6.22)	 Place the thumb and forefinger of one hand under the jaw To prevent air escaping pinch the nose with the hand that is on the casualty's forehead
b. *Mouth-to-nose:* Make an air-tight seal over the victim's nose with your mouth Keep the head back and jaw lifted Close the victim's mouth (Fig. 6.23)	 Place the thumb and forefinger of one hand under the jaw. Check that the other fingers do not press against the throat

Fig. 6.22

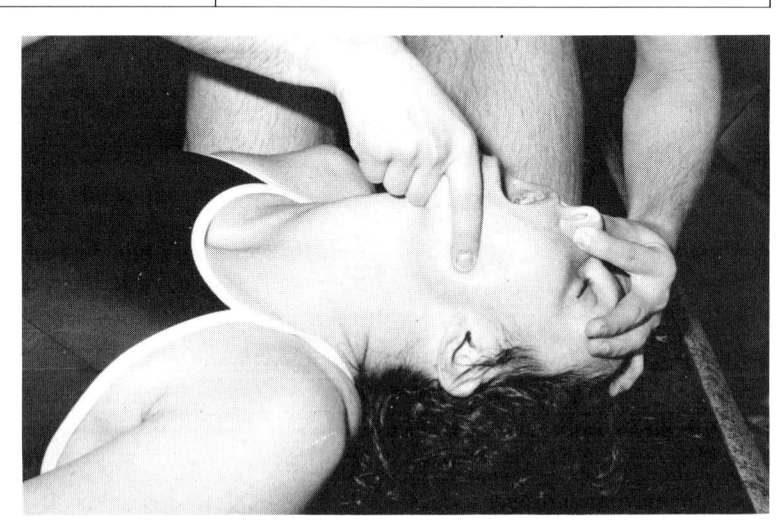

Fig. 6.23

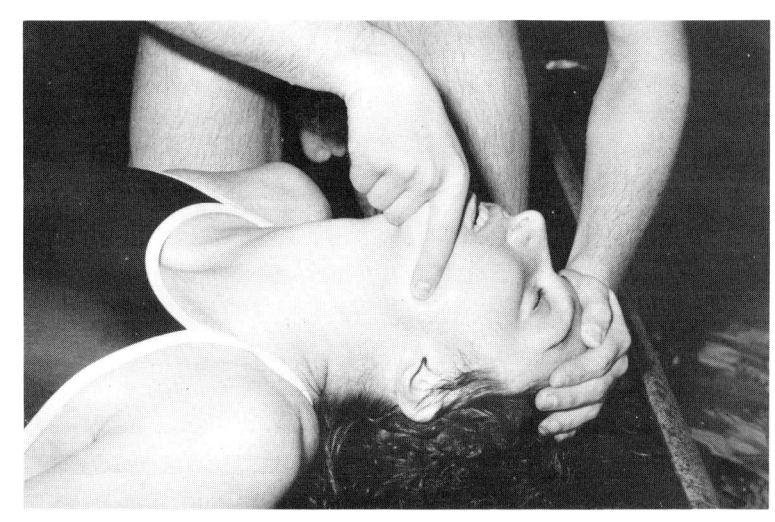

Life saving

Action	Notes
4. *Quick breaths:* Blow into the casualty's mouth or nose for four full breaths	After each blow take your mouth slightly away to get another good breath With infants puff simultaneously into the mouth and nose Check that the chest rises and falls (Fig. 6.24)
Response: a. Casualty's chest will rise and fall and there will be an exchange of air b. Casualty's chest does not rise	Look for the exchange of air. You can watch the chest and listen and even feel the exchange Check for any blockages, ensure the head is in the correct position and that you are making an airtight seal

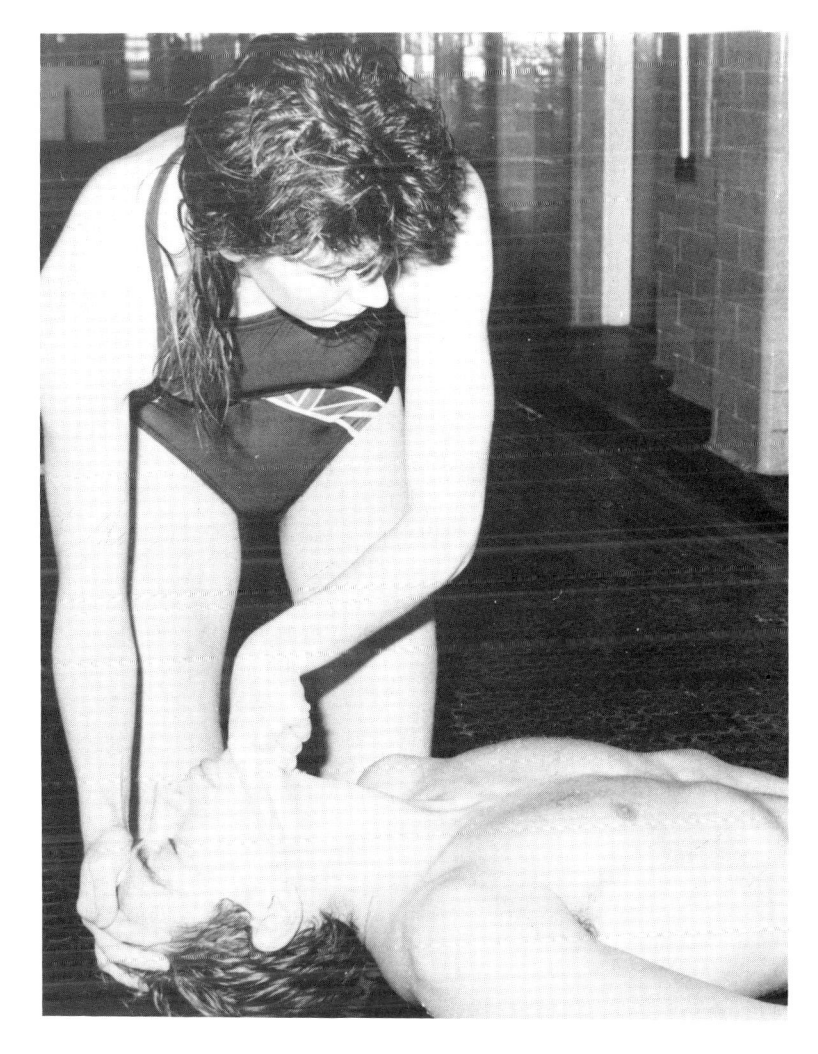

Fig. 6.24

100 Water safety skills – get involved

Action	Notes

5. *Timing:*
  a. Blow into the casualty's mouth or nose every five seconds
 	
  b. The timing for the infant is faster and will be approximately one puff every three seconds
	Remove your mouth after each breath to allow for air exchange and to check for a chest movement
	
	Puff gently
	
	Once the casualty starts breathing: a. continue to watch the casualty, and b. reassure if conscious, and place in the recovery position if still unconscious (Fig. 6.25)

Fig. 6.25

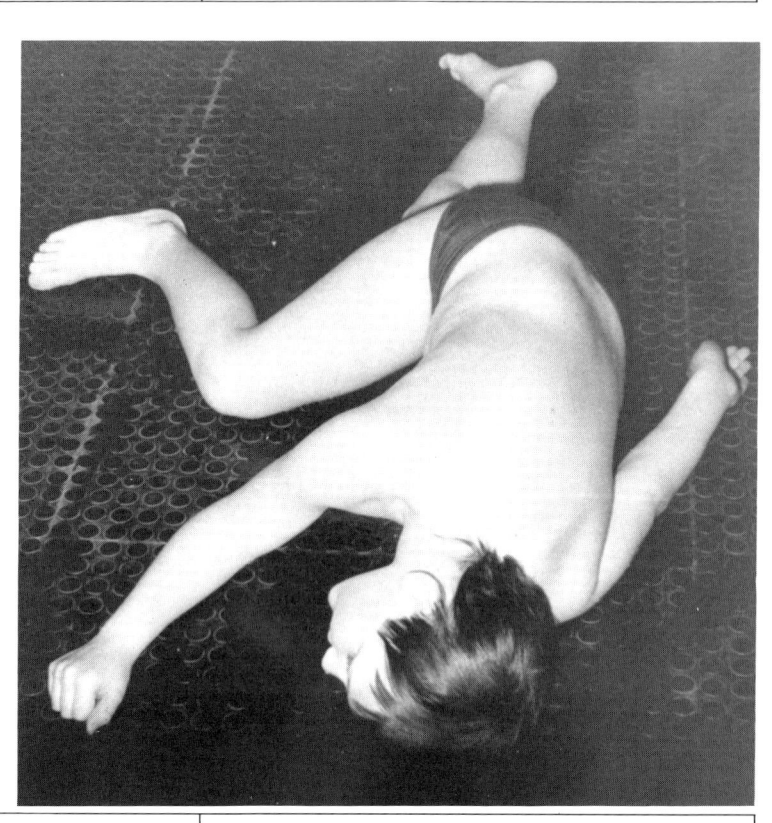

Action	Notes

6. *Shallow water resuscitation:*
  a. Support the casualty with one hand under the far armpit
  b. Tilt the head and keep the mouth closed with the other hand (mouth-to-nose) (Fig. 6.26)
	Ensure that the casualty's face is clear of the water and that the neck is not twisted
	
	Walk to safety as you practise resuscitation

Fig. 6.26

Fig. 6.27

Action	Notes

7. *Aided resuscitation in deep water:*
   a. Place one hand under the neck and grasp the bank, pool side, boat or similar support
   b. Tilt the head and keep the mouth closed with the other hand (mouth-to-nose) (Fig. 6.27)
	Where possible use the thigh to support the victim

8. *Unaided resuscitation in deep water:* Place one hand under the back of the casualty's head, and, with the other hand cupped, lift the jaw and close the mouth (mouth-to-nose) (Fig. 6.28)	Keep the casualty's face above the water Kick hard to raise yourself above the casualty's face Keep the casualty moving Inflate once every ten seconds This is a difficult practice and it can only be carried out by the very competent and experienced pupil

102 Water safety skills – get involved

Fig. 6.28

Action	Notes

9. *When practising resuscitation:*
   a. Breathe out past the victim's far cheek with land resuscitation
   b. Breathe out on the victim's forehead with water resuscitation
	Practise on a manikin wherever possible

10. *General:*
   a. Start resuscitation as soon as possible
   b. Try and get help from a relief resuscitator
   c. Send someone away to telephone for medical help
   d. Get another person to ensure that you have plenty of space in which to work if people are crowding round
   e. Keep checking the pulse in the neck	

Note: for greater detail on expired air resuscitation (EAR) and information about external chest compression (ECC) refer to *Resucitation and First Aid* (1986) by the Royal Life Saving Society, U.K.

Application – make it active

7

Starting competitive swimming

Front start (conventional)

Take your marks

The swimmer steps forwards and places the feet hip width apart with the toes curled over the pool side or starting block (Fig. 7.1).

Starting signal

Overbalance – swing the arms forwards – drive outwards – keep the head between the arms – tense in flight and on entry

During the arm swing stage of the dive a circular backswing may be performed or a straight back and forwards movement. Sometimes the arms are placed behind the hips at the start and, on the starting signal, a short upwards action followed by a vigorous swing forwards is made. The angle of entry is quite narrow to the water surface. However, the breaststroker enters at a slightly steeper angle than the butterflyer and the front crawler enters nearest to the horizontal.

Grab start

Take your marks

The swimmer steps forwards and places the feet close together with the toes curled over the poolside or starting block. The front of the block is grasped either outside the feet or between the feet (Fig. 7.2) but sometimes the side of the block is held (Fig. 7.3).

Starting signal

Pull the body downwards and forwards – keep the head down – swing the arms forwards – keep the head between the arms – tense in flight and on entry

Fig. 7.1

104 Application – make it active

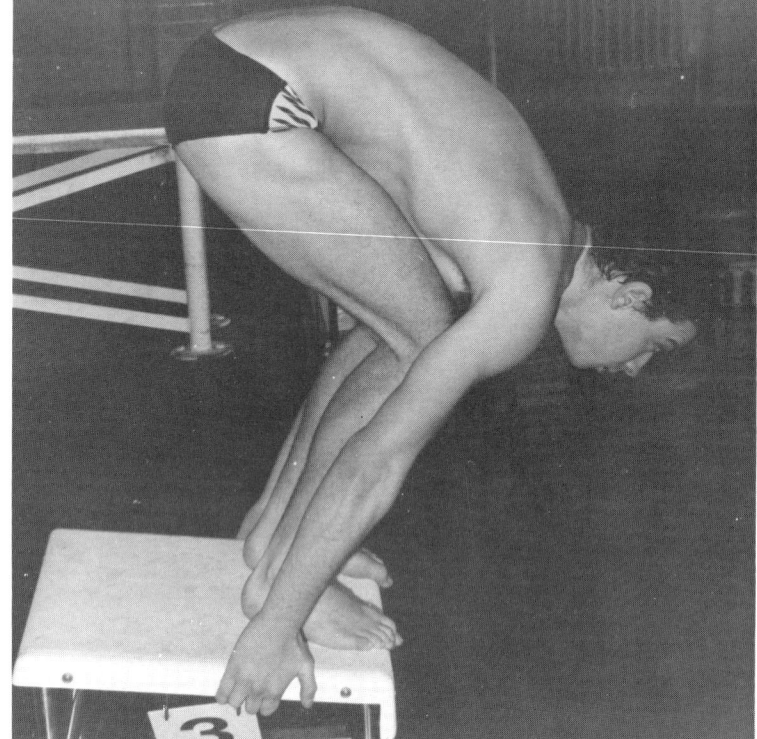

Fig. 7.2. (a)

Fig. 7.2. (b)

Fig. 7.3

Glide, pull and surface (conventional and grab starts)

Although the swimmer using the grab start will enter more quickly and closer to the block, the glide, pull and surfacing techniques will be similar. Once the swimmer has slowed down to swimming speed during the glide, the front crawler will KICK and PULL with one arm to surface and the butterflyer will KICK down and PULL to surface. The breaststroker will PULL to the hips, GLIDE, recover the legs and KICK and STRETCH to surface; the head must break the surface of the water during the first part of the second arm stroke.

Back stroke start

Starting position
The swimmer overgrasps the block handholds, trough or rail.

Take your marks
The swimmer pulls into the block (Fig. 7.4).

Starting signal
Lift the body upwards and outwards – look upwards and backwards – swing the arms sideways and backwards – stretch and slightly arch the back – enter through the fingertips

Glide, pull and surface
Once the swimmer has slowed down to swimming speed during the glide, the back crawler will KICK and PULL with one arm to surface. Some swimmers use a dolphin kick rather than a crawl action and they delay the surfacing.

Butterfly and breast stroke turns

Approach
The swimmer touches the wall with both hands simultaneously and with the shoulders in the horizontal plane (Fig. 7.5).

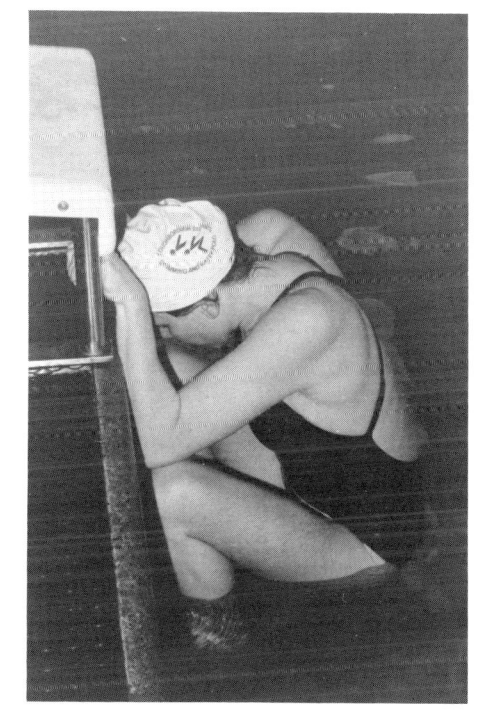

Fig. 7.4

Fig. 7.5

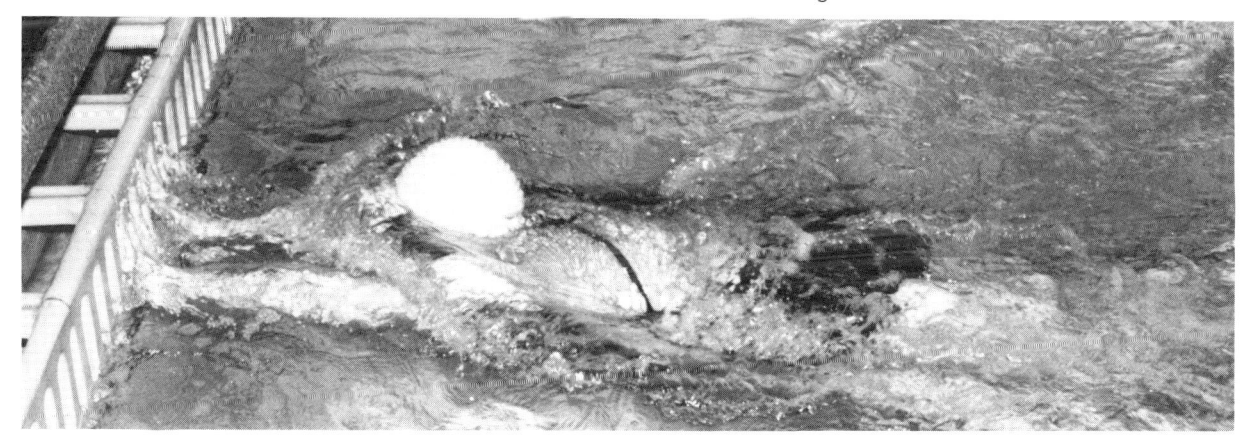

106 Application – make it active

Turn

Bend the arms – look in the new direction – tuck the legs – move on to the side – sink on the side – move the hands to a bent position beyond the head

Push, glide, pull and surface

Push on to the front – stretch from the fingertips to the toes – glide – pull to the hips – glide – recover the legs – kick and stretch to surface (Breast stroke)

Note: the head must break the surface of the water during the first part of the second arm stroke.

Push on to the front – stretch from the fingertips to the toes – glide – move the legs upwards – kick downwards and pull to surface (Butterfly)

Lateral spin turns: head out and head under (front crawl)

Approach

The swimmer stretches the leading arm towards the pool side and touches with the palm of the hand flat against the wall just below the water surface (Fig. 7.6)

Fig. 7.6. (a) and (b)

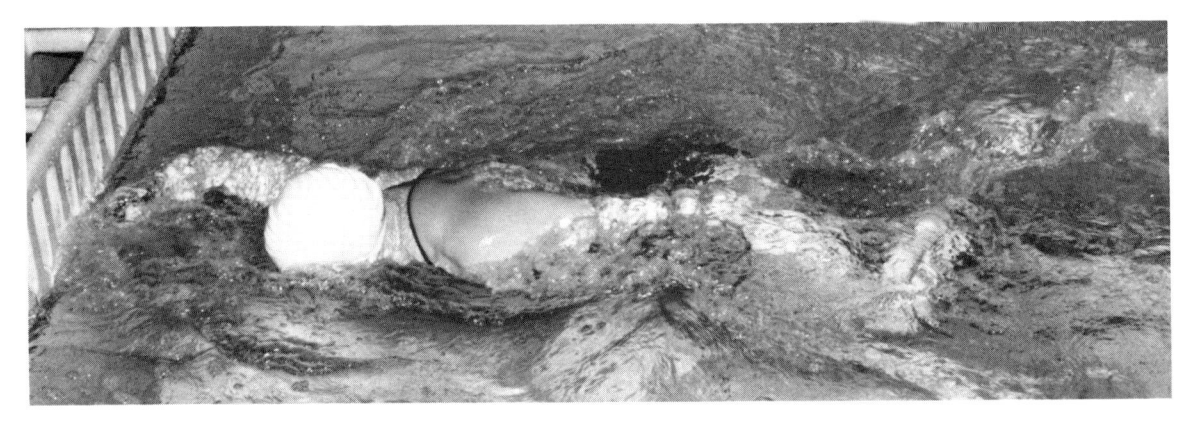

Turn

Bend the arm – turn away from the touching arm – tuck the legs – spin – move the hands to a bent position beyond the head

Push, glide, pull and surface

Push and stretch from the fingertips to the toes – glide – kick and pull with one arm to surface

Throw-away turn (front crawl)

Approach

The swimmer stretches the leading arm towards the pool side and rolls on to that side (Fig. 7.7)

Fig. 7.7

Turn

Bend the arm – turn away from the touching arm – tuck the legs – swing the contact arm over the surface – sink

Push, glide, pull and surface

Push and stretch from the fingertips to the toes – glide – kick and pull with one arm to surface

Twist and somersault turn (front crawl)

Approach

The swimmer stretches the leading arm towards the pool side and rolls on to that side.

108 Application – make it active

Fig. 7.8

Turn (Fig. 7.8)
Bend the arm and twist on to the back – take the head back – tuck the legs – perform a half-somersault

Push, glide, pull and surface
Push and stretch from the fingertips to the toes – glide – kick and pull with one arm to surface

Tumble turn (front crawl)

Approach
The swimmer pulls the leading arm to the side of the body and starts the turn just over one metre from the wall.

Turn (Fig. 7.9)
Drop the head and shoulders – dolphin kick downwards – get the hips upwards – tuck the legs – twist onto the side

Push, glide, pull and surface
Push on to the front – stretch from the fingertips to the toes – glide – kick and pull with one arm to surface

Fig. 7.9. (a)

Starting competitive swimming 109

Fig. 7.9. (b)

Fig. 7.9. (c)

Fig. 7.9. (d)

Fig. 7.9. (e)

110 Application – make it active

Back crawl spin turns: head out and head under

Approach

In both turns the swimmer stretches the leading arm towards the wall and touches the wall with the palm flat against the wall (Fig. 7.10).

Turn

Bend the arm – turn towards the touching arm – tuck the legs – spin – move the hands to a bent position beyond the head

With the 'head out' turn, the legs are mostly below the water surface, whereas in the 'head under' turn, the lower legs and knees are mainly clear of the water surface.

Push, glide, pull and surface

Push and stretch from the fingertips to the toes – glide – kick and pull with one arm to surface

Fig. 7.10. (a) and (b)

Starting competitive swimming

Activity	Practices	Progress report

Front start (conventional)	1. Dive and glide as far as possible
	2. *Front crawl:*
	   a. Dive, glide, kick and then pull
	   b. Dive, glide, kick and pull simultaneously
	3. *Butterfly dolphin:*
	   a. Dive, glide, kick and then pull
	   b. Dive, glide, kick and pull simultaneously
	4. *Breast stroke:*
	   a. Dive, glide, pull and then kick
	   b. Dive, glide, pull, glide, kick and glide
	
	Variations:
	   a. Try a circular backswing start
	   b. Try a straight backswing start
	   c. Try an arms back – swing forwards start
	   d. Practise each of these starts from a block
		Practise in deep water only
		
		Can you:
		dive and glide more than 5 m?
		
		dive and glide further with one particular start?
		
		What is the furthest distance you can dive and glide?
		
		Can you:
		feel that you are gliding quickly after the dive?
		
		keep the head between the arms?
		
		Which start do you find the easiest?

Grab start	Practise as above	Did you hit the water surface sooner using a grab start?
Flight (all starts)	1. Practise jumping into the water with the arms stretched above the head 2. Practise pushing and gliding from the pool side in a stretched position	Check that the head is protected between the arms
Entry (all starts)		Check that the arms stay stretched and do not bend on entry

Glide, pull and surface	Practise pushing and gliding from the pool side and stroking to the surface
	
	Variations:
	   a. Try all three strokes
	   b. In breast stroke try a bent arm pull beneath the body and a straight arm pull to the side
	   c. In front crawl and butterfly dolphin breathe on the second arm pull
		Did you:
		begin the stroke as you started slowing down from the glide?
		feel that you moved smoothly into the stroke?
		
		How far are you travelling underwater?

Application – make it active

Activity	Practices	Progress report
Back stroke start	Practise starting holding on to the pool side *Variations:* a. Try 1. a straight arm, and 2. a bent arm swing b. Try 1. a low, and 2. a high arm swing c. Try a staggered foot position on the wall d. Try a back stroke start from a starting block	*Did you:* have a firm foothold? swing the arms vigorously?
Flight Entry	Practise from a starting block *Variations:* a. Try looking backwards for entry b. Aim to get the body and most of the legs out of the water	*Can you:* arch over the water surface? get your hips over the water surface? Does it feel like a back dive? *Did you:* enter through the fingertips? keep the hips up?
Glide, pull and surface	Push off from the pool side with the arms extended beyond the head *Variations:* a. Glide to the surface b. Try a kick and a double arm pull to the surface c. Try a kick and a single arm pull to the surface d. Try 1. a bent arm, and 2. a straight arm pull e. Try a dolphin leg movement before pulling	Do you prefer to make the first pull with the left or right arm? *Did you:* remember to blow out through the nose? move from the glide to the stroke smoothly?
Breast stroke and butterfly dolphin open turns	Practise swimming and turning into the wall from a distance of 5 metres *Variations:* a. Turn by holding onto the trough or rail b. Turn by placing the hands flat against the wall c. Practise taking one hand away from the wall as quickly as possible d. Try 1. sinking on the front, and 2. on the side	An uneven touch is permitted *Did you:* touch with both hands simultaneously? touch with both arms extended? release the arms before the feet were placed on the wall?

Starting competitive swimming

Activity	Practices	Progress report
Glide, pull and surface	Practise pushing and gliding from the pool side *Variations:* a. Try a long deep glide (at a depth of about half a metre) b. Try gliding, pulling and gliding c. Try gliding, pulling and gliding, kicking to the surface d. Try a bent arm pull beneath the body and a straight arm pull to the side	*Did you:* glide in a streamlined position? feel the surge forwards as you pulled? glide after the pull? begin the stroke as you started slowing down from the glide? break the surface with your head as you started the second stroke?
Lateral spin turns (front crawl)	Practise swimming and turning into the wall from a distance of 5 metres *Variations:* Try turning with 1. the left arm and 2. the right arm Try turning with 1. the head up and 2. the head down	*Did you:* change direction without stopping? take a breath before you turned? The spin can be made with the head up or the head down *Did you:* spin close to the surface?
Throw-away turn (front crawl)	Practise swimming and turning into the wall from a distance of 5 metres *Variations:* Try turning with 1. the left arm and 2. the right arm	Did you approach the wall quickly? Can you turn with either hand? *Did you:* feel the pendulum movement? get your trunk and head beneath the surface? get the contact hand into the water quickly? get a firm footing on the wall?
Twist and somersault (front crawl)	1. Push off from the pool side on the back, glide and then perform a back somersault 2. Push off from the pool side on the front, perform a half twist on to the back and then a somersault 3. Practise swimming into the wall from a distance of 5 metres and just twisting and somersaulting	Practise in deep water only Turn on to the back (or partly on to the back) before touching the wall *Can you:* approach, twist, somersault, in a continuous movement?

114 Application – make it active

Activity	Practices	Progress report
Tumble turn (front crawl)	1. Push off from the pool side with the hands by the side and perform a tucked somersault *Variations:* a. Try one or two butterfly dolphin leg movements before somersaulting b. Try pushing downwards with the hands as the somersault is performed c. Try starting the somersault in a piked position and tucking late 2. Practise swimming and turning into the wall from a distance of 5 metres *Variations:* a. Try somersaulting in a loose tuck position and pushing away on the back b. Try starting the somersault in a pike position and tucking late	Practise in deep water only Remember that you only have to touch with the feet *Can you:* judge the distance from the wall? perform a downward butterfly dolphin kick as you somersault? move smoothly into the twist from the somersault?
Push (all front crawl turns)	Push off from the pool side and get into a stretched position as soon as possible	*Did you:* get away from the wall quickly? push away from a semi-tucked position?
Glide, pull and surface (all front crawl turns)	1. Push off from the pool side on the side and move on to the front during the glide *Variations:* a. Try gliding and kicking to the surface b. Try gliding, kicking and pulling with one arm to surface c. Turn to breathe on the second arm pull 2. Practise swimming into the wall from a distance of 5 metres, turning and stroking to the surface	*Did you:* begin the stroke as you started slowing down from the glide? feel that you moved smoothly into the stroke? How far are you travelling under water?

Starting competitive swimming

Activity	Practices	Progress report
Back crawl spin turns	1. Practise spinning on the back in the shallow end of the pool 2. Practise pushing from the pool side, gliding and then spinning on the back 3. Practise swimming into the wall from a distance of 5 metres and turning *Variations:* a. Try kicking into the turn with the contact arm extended beyond the head b. Try turning with the head out of the water and the head submerged	Remember to stay on your back Can you turn to the left and to the right? With practice the legs can be lifted sideways over the water surface If the legs are brought over the surface the trunk will be forced under the water
Push	Push off from the pool side on the back with the arms extended beyond the head	Stretch the arms as early as possible
Glide, pull and surface	Push off from the pool side on the back and hold a short glide before surfacing *Variations:* a. Try a kick and a double arm pull to the surface b. Try a kick and a single arm pull to the surface c. Try 1. a bent arm pull, and 2. a straight arm pull d. Try a dolphin leg movement before pulling	Do you prefer the single or double arm pull?

Simple schedules

Strokes: front crawl, back crawl, breast stroke, butterfly dolphin
Length of pool: 25 metres
Width of pool: 10 metres
Equipment: kicking boards, pull-buoys, sweep-hand clock
Notes: when distances are broken up (e.g. 6 × 25 metres, 15 seconds rest between each length) repetitions should be swum at a faster speed

Schedule 1 (widths)
Take 30 seconds rest between each section. Select your best stroke.

1. 8 widths/full stroke/continuous
2. 6 widths/pulling/continuous
3. 4 widths/kicking/4 × 10 metres: 15 seconds rest between each width
4. 6 widths/full stroke/continuous

Select a second stroke

5. 6 widths/full stroke/continuous

Total 30 widths (300 metres)

116 Application – make it active

Schedule 2 (widths)

Take 30 seconds rest between each section. Select a first and a second stroke.

1. 8 widths/full stroke (1st stroke)/continuous
2. 8 widths/full stroke (2nd stroke)/continuous
3. 4 widths/pulling (1st stroke)/continuous
4. 4 widths/kicking (1st stroke)/4 × 10 metres: 15 seconds rest between each width
5. 4 widths/pulling (2nd stroke)/continuous
6. 4 widths/kicking (2nd stroke)/4 × 10 metres: 15 seconds rest between each width
7. 4 widths/full stroke (1st stroke)/2 × 20 metres: 15 seconds rest between each 20 metres
8. 4 widths/full stroke (2nd stroke)/2 × 20 metres: 15 seconds rest between each 20 metres

Total 40 widths (400 metres)

Schedule 3 (widths)

Take 30 seconds rest between each section.

1. 6 widths/back crawl/continuous
2. 6 widths/breast stroke/continuous
3. 6 widths/front crawl/continuous
4. 6 widths/medley (3 strokes)*/2 × 30 metres: 15 seconds rest between each 30 metres
5. 12 widths/4 widths continuously on each of the three strokes*/3 × 40 metres: 15 seconds rest between each 40 metres
6. 12 widths/4 widths on each of the three strokes/continuous
7. 2 widths/butterfly dolphin*/continuous

Total 50 widths (500 metres)

* order of strokes: back crawl, breast stroke, front crawl

Schedule 4 (widths)

Take 30 seconds rest between each section.

1. 12 widths/medley*/3 × 40 metres, continuous
2. 8 widths/pulling, medley*/2 × 40 metres/continuous
3. 8 widths/kicking, medley*/2 × 40 metres/continuous
4. 6 widths/butterfly dolphin/6 × 10 metres: 15 seconds rest between each width
5. 6 widths/back crawl/continuous
6. 6 widths/breast stroke/continuous
7. 6 widths/front crawl/continuous
8. 8 widths/medley*/2 × 40 metres fast: 20 seconds rest between each 40 metres

Total 60 widths (600 metres)

*order of strokes: butterfly dolphin, back crawl, breast stroke, front crawl

Schedule 5 (lengths)

Take 1 minute's rest between each section. Select your best stroke.

1. 6 lengths/full stroke/continuous
2. 4 lengths/pulling/continuous
3. 4 lengths/kicking/4 × 25 metres: 20 seconds rest between each length
4. 6 lengths/full stroke/continuous

Starting competitive swimming

5. 6 lengths/full stroke/3 × 50 metres: 30 seconds rest between each 50 metres
6. 6 lengths/full stroke/6 × 25 metres: 15 seconds rest between each length

Total 32 lengths (800 metres)

Schedule 6 (lengths)
Take 1 minute's rest between each section.
1. 8 lengths/back crawl/continuous
2. 8 lengths/front crawl/continuous
3. 6 lengths/pulling, back crawl/3 × 50 metres: 30 seconds rest between each 50 metres
4. 4 lengths/kicking, back crawl/4 × 25 metres: 20 seconds between each length
5. 4 lengths/alternate front crawl and back crawl/continuous
6. 4 lengths/pulling, front crawl/2 × 50 metres: 30 seconds rest between each 50 metres
7. 2 lengths/kicking, front crawl/2 × 25 metres: 20 seconds rest between each length
8. 4 lengths/back crawl and front crawl/50 metres back crawl, 50 metres front crawl: 30 seconds rest between each 50 metres

Total 40 lengths (1000 metres)

Schedule 7 (lengths)
Take 1 minute's rest between each section.
1. 10 lengths/front crawl/continuous
2. 8 lengths/breast stroke/continuous
3. 6 lengths/back crawl/continuous
4. 4 lengths/butterfly dolphin/4 × 25 metres: 30 seconds between each length
5. 4 lengths/pulling, medley*/continuous
6. 4 lengths/kicking, medley*/continuous
7. 8 lengths/medley*/50 metres on each stroke/continuous
8. 4 lengths/front crawl/continuous and fast

Total 48 lengths (1200 metres)

*order of strokes: butterfly dolphin, back crawl, breast stroke, front crawl

Schedule 8 (lengths)
Take 1 minute's rest between each section. A front crawl schedule.
1. 8 lengths/full stroke/continuous
2. 8 lengths/pulling/continuous
3. 8 lengths/kicking/continuous
4. 8 lengths/full stroke/2 × 100 metres: 40 seconds rest between each 100 metres
5. 8 lengths/pulling/4 × 50 metres: 20 seconds rest between each 50 metres
6. 8 lengths/kicking/8 × 25 metres: 20 seconds rest between each length
7. 4 lengths/full stroke/4 × 25 metres, fast: 10 seconds rest between each length
8. 4 lengths/full stroke/continuous and slow

Total 56 lengths (1400 metres)

Life saving problems

The teacher sets the problem and the rescuer or rescuers try to solve it in a safe and efficient way.

Problem 1

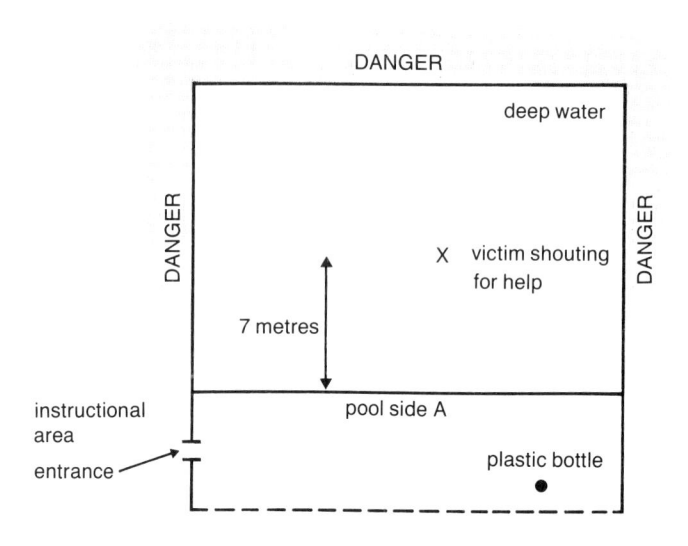

```
                    DANGER
         ┌─────────────────────────┐
         │              deep water │
         │                         │
    D    │                         │  D
    A    │         X  victim shouting  A
    N    │            for help     │  N
    G    │    ↑                    │  G
    E    │ 7 metres                │  E
    R    │    ↓                    │  R
         │                         │
         ├─────pool side A─────────┤
instructional                      │
area                    plastic bottle
         ╷  ╷                  ●   │
entrance ─┘  └─ ─ ─ ─ ─ ─ ─ ─ ─ ─ ─┘
```

Instructions
1. Look at the diagram (cover up 'pool side A').
2. You come in through the gap marked 'entrance'.
3. You may use any equipment found on 'pool side A'.
4. The victim is a weak swimmer who is in difficulty in deep water.
5. You cannot go into the 'danger' areas.
6. Any questions?
7. Go!

A solution (one rescuer)

Did you:
- see the plastic bottle?
- tell the victim to stay calm?
- take careful aim before throwing the bottle?
- throw the bottle to within the victim's reach?
- tell the victim to hold the bottle with two hands and to kick gently?
- assist the victim on to 'pool side A'?
- get the victim away from the water's edge?

Problem 2

```
                         DANGER
               shallow water      deep water
   pool side B
                    20 metres
                   ←———————→ X
   pole                          victim shouting
                                    for help                DANGER

                    15 metres
        float ■    ←———————→ X
                                 very tired swimmer

       ⊢ ↑ ⊢
     entrance        DANGER

   instructional area
```

Instructions
1. Look at the diagram (cover up 'pool side B').
2. You come in through the gap marked 'entrance'.
3. You may use any equipment found on 'pool side B'.
4. There are two victims in deep water – one victim is panicking and shouting for help and the other one is a calm but tired swimmer.
5. You cannot go into the danger areas.
6. Any questions?
7. Go!

A solution (one or two rescuers)

Did you:
- see the pole and float?
- tell the victims to stay calm?
- slip into the water feet first?
- wade in shallow water?
- take aim and throw the float within arm's reach of the tired swimmer?
- tell the tired swimmer to hold the float and kick towards shallow water?
- swim with the pole to the shouting victim?
- keep your distance from the shouting victim?
- tell the shouting victim to hold the pole with two hands?
- encourage the shouting victim to hold the pole with extended arms, keep the head up and to kick gently?
- tow with a straight arm?
- watch the victims constantly?
- encourge the victims to walk on reaching shallow water?
- assist the victims on to 'pool side B'?
- get the victims away from the water's edge?

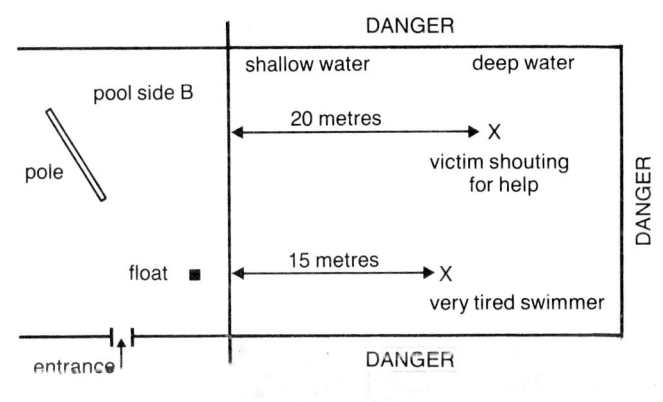

Problem 3

```
                    |         DANGER
                    |  shallow water      deep water
    buoyant ring    |
        O           |
                    |              X
    pool side B     |   20 metres      victims
                    |  <----------->   shouting
                    |                  for help
          float     |              X
             ■      |
         ┤ ↑ ├      |         DANGER
    entrance
    instructional area
```

Instructions
1. Look at the diagram (cover up 'pool side B').
2. You come in through the gap marked 'entrance'.
3. You may use any equipment found on 'pool side B'.
4. There are two victims panicking and shouting for help in deep water.
5. You cannot go in the danger areas.
6. Any questions?
7. Go!

A solution (one or two rescuers)
Did you:
- see the float and buoyant ring?
- tell the victims to stay calm?
- slip into the water feet first?
- wade in shallow water?
- take aim and throw the float to one victim and the buoyant ring to the other?
- throw within the victims' reach?
- keep the victims apart?
- tell the victims to hold the aids with two hands and kick gently towards shallow water?
- keep your distance from the victims?
- watch the victims constantly?
- encourage the victims to walk on reaching shallow water?
- assist the victims on to 'pool side B'?
- get the victims away from the water's edge?

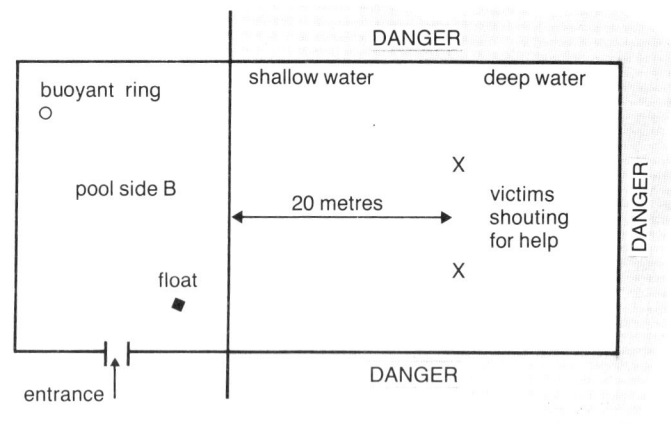

Problem 4

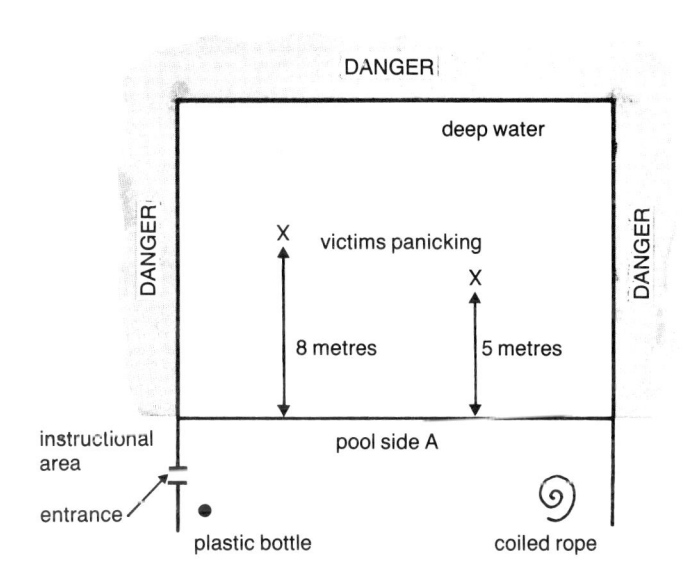

[Diagram: A rectangular pool with "DANGER" labeled on top, left, and right sides. Top edge labeled "deep water". Two victims marked X are panicking, one 8 metres from pool side A, another 5 metres from pool side A. Bottom edge is "pool side A". Outside the pool at bottom-left is the "instructional area" with "entrance", a "plastic bottle", and to the right a "coiled rope".]

Instructions
1. Look at the diagram (cover up 'pool side B').
2. You come in through the gap marked 'entrance'.
3. You may use any equipment found on 'pool side B'.
4. There are two victims panicking and shouting for help in deep water.
5. You cannot go in the danger areas.
6. Any questions?
7. Go!

A solution (one or two rescuers)

Did you:
- see the plastic bottle and coiled rope?
- tell the victims to stay calm?
- throw the plastic bottle to the nearer victim?
- throw the rope to the further victim?
- tell the nearer victim to hold the plastic bottle with two hands and kick gently towards 'pool side A'?
- throw the plastic bottle and rope within the victims' reach?
- keep the victims apart?
- watch the victims constantly?
- assist the victims on to 'pool side A'?
- get the victims away from the water's edge?

Problem 5

```
                    |         DANGER
        pool side B | shallow water    deep water
                    |    20 metres
                    |   ←————————→  X victim
                    |                  shouting
        float       |                  for help
         ■          |    15 metres
                    |   ←—————→    X unconscious
                    |                  victim
    ————————| ↑ |———|————————————————————————
        entrance              DANGER

    instructional area
```

Instructions
1. Look at the diagram (cover up 'pool side B').
2. You come in through the gap marked 'entrance'.
3. You may use any equipment found on 'pool side B'.
4. There are two victims in deep water – one victim is panicking and shouting and the other one is unconscious and breathing but becomes conscious as the pool side is reached.
5. You cannot go in the danger areas.
6. Any questions?
7. Go!

A solution (one or two rescuers)

Did you:
- see the float?
- slip into the water feet first?
- wade in shallow water?
- tell the shouting victim to stay calm?
- wade towards the unconscious victim and throw the float towards the shouting victim?
- approach the unconscious victim from behind?
- tell the shouting victim to hold the float with two hands and kick gently towards shallow water?
- keep the unconscious victim's face above the water?
- use a straight arm or bent arm tow?
- watch the shouting victim constantly?
- keep your distance from the shouting victim?
- encourage the shouting victim to walk on reaching shallow water?
- assist the victims on to 'pool side B'?
- get the victims away from the water's edge?

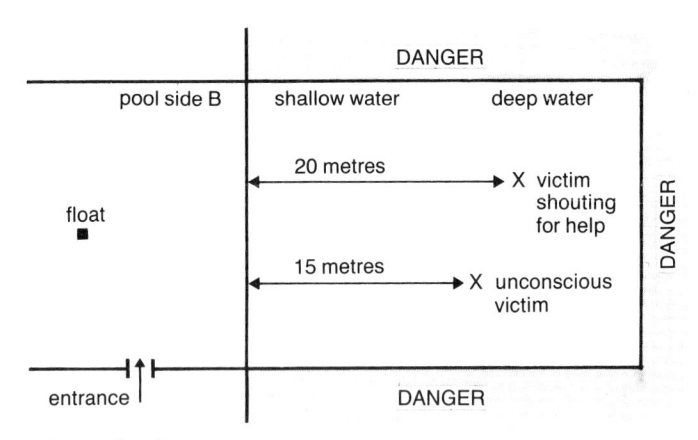

Problem 6

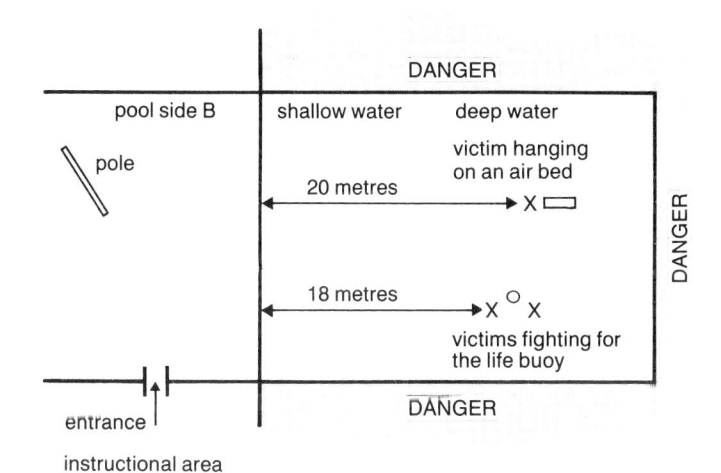

```
                    |  DANGER
    pool side B     | shallow water    deep water
      \ pole        |                  victim hanging
       \            |    20 metres     on an air bed
                    |←──────────────→ x ▭
                    |
                    |    18 metres
                    |←──────────────→ x ○ x
                    |                 victims fighting for
                    |                 the life buoy
   ──┤ ├────────────|  DANGER
   entrance ↑
   instructional area
```

Instructions
1. Look at the diagram (cover up 'pool side B').
2. You come in through the gap marked 'entrance'.
3. You may use any equipment found on 'pool side B'.
4. There are three panicking and shouting victims in deep water.
5. You cannot go in the danger areas.
6. Any questions?
7. Go!

A solution (two or three rescuers)
Did you:
- see the pole?
- slip into the water feet first?
- wade in shallow water?
- tell the victims to stay calm?
- tell the air-bed victim to kick gently towards the shallow end?
- approach the shouting victims carefully?
- keep your distance from the shouting victims?
- try and persuade one shouting victim to hold the pole?
- tell the shouting victim to hold the pole with two hands, keep the head up and kick gently?
- tell the life-buoy victim to kick gently towards the shallow end?
- keep the victims apart?
- watch the victims constantly?
- encourage the victims to walk on reaching shallow water?
- assist the victims on to 'pool side B'?
- get the victims away from the water's edge?

More practices and the development of a game form (more advanced swimmer)

Practices

Can you:
- swim behind a partner performing breast stroke keeping in time?
- swim by the side of a partner performing breast stroke keeping in time?
- swim in time with your partner on front crawl?
- swim in time with your partner on back crawl?
- swim in time with your partner when using a breast stroke with a long glide?
- swim in time with your partner when using a slow bent arm recovery on front crawl?
- swim in time with your partner when using a slow bent arm recovery on back crawl?
- change from breast stroke to back crawl in time with your partner?
- change from back crawl to front crawl in time with your partner?
- change direction and stay in time with your partner when using a breast stroke?
- perform a sequence in time with your partner using two strokes and two changes of direction?
- perform any other skills in time with your partner?
- face your partner while treading water and mirror any arm actions?
- face your partner while treading water and mirror any arm actions and body turns?
- perform a sequence with your partner involving two strokes, two changes of direction, six arm actions and two turns while treading water?

As the pupils gain greater control of their movements, sequences involving groups of three or four pupils can be attempted.

Game form

Rope off areas of approximately 10 metres by 5 metres in the deeper water.

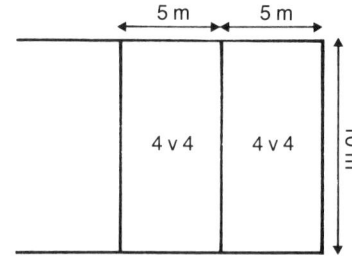

```
     5 m     5 m
   |-----|-----|
   |     |     | ↑
   |     |     |
   | 4v4 | 4v4 | 10 m
   |     |     |
   |     |     | ↓
```

More practices and the development of a game form 125

Equipment	– One ball for each game
Teams	– Four pupils in each team
General rules	– Play the ball only while swimming and not when holding the pool side or rope
	– Play the ball and not the person
	– Play the ball with one or two hands but do not take the ball under the water surface
	– If any rule is broken a free throw is taken by the opposition at the point of infringement
Starting the game	– Each team lines up anywhere in their own half of the pool and a member of one team starts the game by throwing the ball backwards from the centre
Scoring	– A player scores by holding the ball for a moment against the opponents' goal line
	– When a goal is scored the players go back to their own half and a member of the team that has had a goal scored against it re-starts by throwing the ball backwards from the centre
	– A rebound off the goal line is not a goal and a free throw is given to the defending team from the goal line
Safety	– If the game is played for 10 minutes (i.e. 2 halves of 5 minutes), the pupils must be capable of working in deep water for that length of time

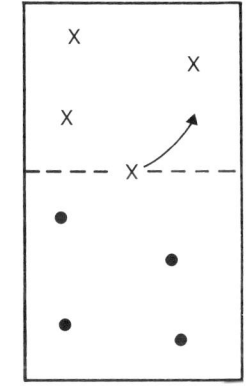

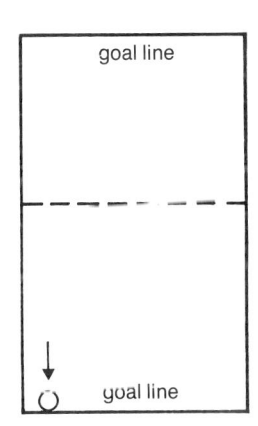

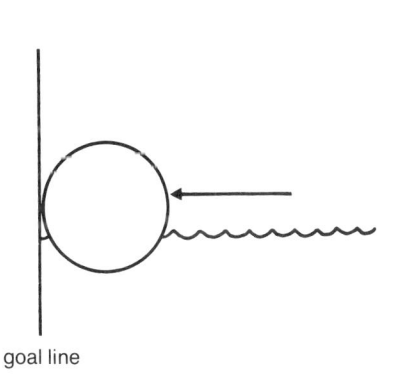

126 Application – make it active

- The game must be supervised closely by a qualified swimming teacher
- The game can either be controlled by a referee or by two team captains

Once the pupils can play the game safely and with control it can be developed in the following ways over a period of weeks:

Developmental stages

1. General rules

   Scoring

   Play the ball with one hand only
   - A player scores by throwing the ball into any one of three hoops placed upon the pool side at the opponents' goal line
   - A goal can only be scored when the player is in the opponents' half

2. General rules

   Scoring

   - A goalkeeper (G.K.) is named and that person may play the ball with one or two hands
   - A player scores by throwing the ball and hitting the pool side between two markers placed on the pool side
   - A goal can only be scored when the player is in the opponents' half

   markers

3. General rules
   – No pushing off from the pool side in order to play the ball
   – If goalkeepers deflect the ball over their own goal line but outside the markers, a corner is awarded at the side of the pool, two metres from the goal line
   – A goal cannot be scored direct from a corner

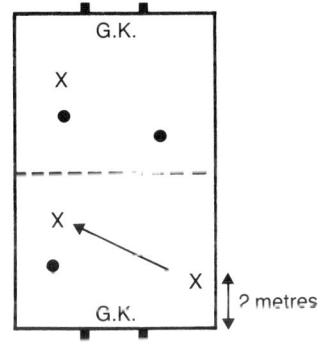

4. Increase the playing area and the number of pupils in a team, and allow the pupils to develop their own positional and game strategies.

   Game forms give the pupils:
   - an experience of playing to the rules;
   - leadership opportunities to those who referee or act as captains (rotate these positions);
   - a chance to develop co-operative behaviour;
   - the opportunity to make decisions in the development of positional game strategies.

8 Lesson plans – get variety

A confidence lesson (non-swimmer)

Plan
Objectives
Main teaching points
Equipment

Phase
Organisation
Entry
Progress
Game form
Revision

Approximate timing
Phases one and two should take one-fifth of the allocated time, phase three two-fifths, phases four and five one-fifth each.

Plan

Objectives
1. Hold the side of the pool (with or without a supportive aid), bring the legs to the surface and lower the feet to the bottom of the pool.
2. Walk in the shallow end of the pool for a distance of at least 10 metres using an arm movement.
3. Propel yourself more than 5 metres while being supported by a ring
4. Perform any one trick using a piece of equipment (e.g. step out of a floating hoop).

Main teaching points
'grasp over the rail' (or through).
'slide the feet along' (i.e. the bottom of the pool).

'keep shoulders below the water surface' (i.e. whenever possible).
'stay close to your partner' (i.e. all the time).

Equipment

rings
hoops
soft balls
markers indicating five and ten metres
lane rope

Organisation

a. Pair the pupils so that there are always two pupils working close together in the water.
b. Define the working area by placing a lane rope across the pool.
c. Work in the shallow end of the pool.
d. Carry out the required hygienic practices (e.g. use of toilet, showers and footbath).

Phase

Entry

a. Enter down the steps.
b. Hold on to the rail if necessary.
c. Stay close to your partner.
d. Hold on to the rail (or trough) once you are in the water.
e. Walk and/or jump up and down while holding on to the rail (or trough).

Progress

Hold on to the rail (or trough) with both hands
Can you:
- slide your feet backwards and forwards and remain on the spot?
- walk sideways?
- slide your feet backwards and forwards and remain on the spot while facing away from the side of the pool?
- jump up and down in the water?
- walk up and down the wall?

Assessment   Can you bring your feet to the surface and lower them down again?

Hold onto the rail (or trough) with one hand
Can you:
- walk forwards?
- walk backwards?
- walk with your feet turned outwards?
- walk with your feet turned inwards?
- pull with the free hand?

Walking hand-in-hand with your partner
Can you:
- walk forwards?
- walk backwards?
- move round in a circle?
- walk behind your partner?

<u>Assessment</u> Can you walk 10 metres or more?

Taking the body weight on a ring
Can you:
- move round in a circle?
- move forwards?
- move backwards?
- move sideways?
- pull with both hands together?
- pull with one hand and then the other?

<u>Assessment</u> Can you propel yourself more than 5 metres in a supportive ring?

Game form
Give each pair a soft ball and a hoop
Can you:
- throw the ball into a floating hoop?
- throw the ball through a hoop placed vertically?
- get in and out of a floating hoop (you can hold on to the side of the pool or get your partner to help)?
- invent a game with a ball?

<u>Assessment</u> Can you show me what you can do with a hoop and/or ball?

Revision
a. Practise movements holding on to the side of the pool or a partner.
b. Practise movements using a supportive ring.
c. Play with the soft ball and hoop.

Obviously there will be a range of ability even at the non-swimmer level, so choose the appropriate questions and adapt the language according to the age. The four objectives would not necessarily have to be achieved by all, but make sure everyone achieves at least one objective.

If you have 40 minutes water time and 16 non-swimmers it is better to take two 20-minute lessons with eight in each. It is easier to keep eight individuals in your sight, to keep their attention and to motivate them continually.

A very nervous non-swimmer will need a great deal of individual attention and this may entail the teacher taking the student on a one-to-one basis outside the normal class situation.

An early stroke lesson (elementary swimmer)

Plan
Objectives
Main teaching points
Equipment

Phase
Organisation
Warm up
Stroke development: **a.** ways of moving in the water
b. breast stroke
c. full stroke
Game form
Talk about the session

Approximate timing
Phases one and two should take one-fifth of the allocated time, phase three one-half, phase four one-fifth and phase five one-tenth.

Objectives
1. Find three different ways of swimming in water and swim a minimum of 5 metres with each of these ways.
2. Swim a minimum distance of 5 metres on breast stroke showing good timing (i.e. the kick is made as the arms stretch forwards).
3. Co-operate with others in a game form.
4. Talk about the session with other swimmers and with the teacher.

Main teaching points

General: 'keep the fingers closed'
'keep the wrists firm'
'circle the legs' (breast stroke type movement)
'stretch the legs' (crawl type movement)
'scissor the legs' (side stroke)

Breast stroke: 'circle the legs'
'keep the hands in sight'
'kick as the arms stretch forwards'

Phase

Lesson plans – get variety

Phase

Equipment
lane rope
kick-boards
supportive rings
hoops and soft balls
markers

Organisation
a. Pair the pupils so that there are always two pupils working close together in the water.
b. Define the working area (e.g. a lane rope across the pool).
c. Work in the shallow end of the pool.
d. Place markers on the pool side to indicate 5-metre distances.
e. Explain the meaning of the words simultaneous and alternate in a swimming context.

Warm up
Practise any stroke action that has been learned in a previous lesson.
Can you:
- swim more than five strokes with this action?
- keep both your arms and legs going?
- breathe in and out easily?

Stroke development
a. Ways of moving in the water
Walking in the shallow end.
Can you:
- pull with your arms simultaneously?
- pull with your arms alternately?
- pull and recover your arms beneath the water surface?
- pull and recover your arms over the water surface?
- pull walking backwards?
- pull walking sideways?

Holding a kick-board.
Can you:
- move by circling the legs together?
- move by circling the legs alternately?
- move by kicking the legs up and down simultaneously?
- move by kicking the legs up and down alternately?
- try those kicking movements on your back?

Supported in a ring.
Can you:
- swim co-ordinating a simultaneous leg action with a simultaneous arm movement?
- swim co-ordinating an alternating leg action with an alternating arm movement?
- move by co-ordinating a simultaneous leg action with an alternate arm movement?

- move by co-ordinating an alternate leg action with a simultaneous arm movement?
- try any of these movements on your back or side?

Assessment   Without a ring can you:
- find three ways of swimming in the water?
- swim 5 metres with each of these ways?

b.   Breast stroke

Can you:
- push away from the side of the pool and glide with the arms stretched out beyond the head?
- glide, pull and kick and then glide?

Holding a kick-board.
Can you:
- move by just kicking?
- hold a short glide after each kick?
- kick and glide on your back?

Walk and pull.
Can you:
- feel your hands holding on to the water?
- keep your hands in sight?

c.   Full stroke

Can you:
- glide, pull and kick the arms forwards?
- glide after each kick?

Assessment   Can you travel 5 metres with less than five complete strokes?

Game form

Give a hoop and one soft ball between a group of three subjects

Can you:
- throw to a partner through the hoop?
- take the ball under and pop it up in the hoop?
- swim with the ball through a submerged hoop?
- make up a game?

Talk about the session

All the subjects should be encouraged to talk about the lesson.
Did you:
- manage to find different ways of swimming?
- swim at least 5 metres with each of these ways?
- see other subjects using your ways of swimming?
- swim at least 5 metres using a breast stroke?
- feel your arms moving forwards before you kicked?

A water safety lesson (more advanced swimmer)

Plan

Objectives
Main teaching points
Equipment

Phase

Organisation
Life saving swimming skills
Rescue skills **a.** non-contact towing rescue
             b. straddle entry
             c. a sequence of rescue skills
A task (in pairs)
Talk about the session

Approximate timing

Phase one one-tenth of the allocated time, phase two one-fifth, phase three two-fifths, phase four one-fifth and phase five one-tenth.

Plan

Objectives

1. Swim a minimum of 25 metres using either a side stroke or a life saving kick. (In the former only the leading arm can be used with the kick and in the latter one arm can be used to assist the kick.)
2. Tow a partner a minimum of 10 metres using a non-contact rescue.
3. Perform a straddle entry from the pool side into deep water.
4. Perform a sequence of rescue skills continuously and effectively.
5. Organise and perform a set task.
6. Work with others and discuss the session.

Main teaching points

Strokes:	side stroke: 'scissor and straighten the legs'
	life saving kick: 'sweep the lower legs round and together'
	approach stroke: 'focus on the victim'
Rescue:	non-contact rescue: 'keep the arm straight'

A water safety lesson

Straddle entry: stance: 'get a firm grip with the front foot'
flight: 'hold a running position'
water reaches the waist: 'scissor the legs and push down with the hands'

Equipment
1-metre length poles
lane rope
towels

Organisation
a. Pair the pupils.
b. Define the working area by placing a lane rope across the pool.
c. Work in the deep end of the pool.

Life saving swimming skills
Can you:
- swim a width on side stroke?
- swim a width using a life saving kick and sculling with the hands?
- imagine that you are towing and that you can only use one arm to assist the kick?
- swim one width on front crawl with the head up?

Assessment   Can you swim for 25 metres on either a side stroke or a life saving kick? (use one arm only to assist propulsion)

Rescue skills
a. Non-contact towing rescue

Practise towing a partner across the width of the pool. Change the position of tower and subject on a regular basis.
Did you:
- approach carefully?
- avoid bodily contact?
- get the victim to turn onto the back?
- get the victim to hold on to one end of the pole close to the chest?
- tow with a rigid arm?
- encourage the subject to kick gently?

Can you:
- keep the subject's face above the water?
- tow smoothly?

Assessment   Can you tow the subject more than 10 metres?

b. Straddle entry
- Practise straddle jumping into deep water.

Phase

Did you:
- jump well out?
- hold the straddle position in flight?
- manage to keep your head above the water all the time?

Can you:
- straddle jump and swim quickly across the width?
- straddle jump, swim across the width and still focus on a point on the pool side?

Assessment   Can you perform an effective straddle entry from the pool side into deep water?

c.   A sequence of rescue skills

Assessment   Can you straddle jump, swim 10 metres with a front crawl head-up approach, collect a pole from the pool side and tow a subject for 10 metres using a non-contact tow?

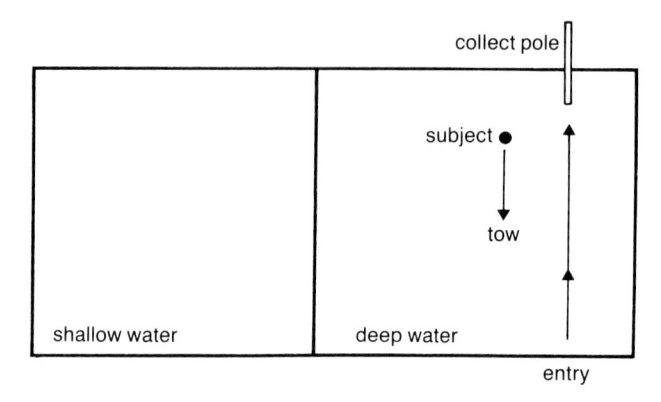

A task (in pairs)

Work out a sequence of rescue and swimming skills that involves:
a. a straddle entry
b. swimming the side stroke, life saving kick and front crawl (head up) carrying a towel
c. a non-contact tow
d. taking two to three minutes to complete

Assessment   Can you perform this sequence effectively and with speed?

Talk about the session

All participants should be encouraged to talk about the lesson. What did you learn about water safety?

A competitive swimming lesson (more advanced swimmer)

Plan

Objectives
Main teaching points
Equipment

Phase

Organisation
Warm up
Training schedule: **a.** fartlek training
                      b. interval training: part and full stroke practices
                      c. 'catch-up' with hand paddles
Variety
Talk about the session

Approximate timing

An average swimmer could complete the schedule in approximately 50 minutes.

Plan

Objectives
1. Complete the training schedule on front crawl.
2. Spend time practising a second stroke.
3. Train with others and discuss the session.

Main teaching points
    Strokes: front crawl – 'lift the elbow and trail the hand' (recovery)
                          'keep the elbow up' (pull)
                          second stroke- 'keep the wrists firm' (pull)

Equipment
lane ropes
kick-boards
pull-buoys
hand paddles
clock with a sweep-second hand
blackboard(s)

Phase

Organisation
a. Identify the swimmers' ability.
b. Lanes 1 and 5 for the weaker swimmers, lanes 2, 3 and 4 for the stronger swimmers.

c. Direction of swimming:
   lane 1 – clockwise
   lane 2 – anti-clockwise
   lane 3 – clockwise
   lane 4 – anti-clockwise
   lane 5 – clockwise.
d. Check that any adult swimmers are periodically examined by doctors and that they are fit enough to take part in the training lesson.
e. Write the schedule on a blackboard and place so that all can see.

Warm up

All participants swim slowly and continuously for 6 minutes. The first length will be on breast stroke, the second length on back crawl and the third length on front crawl; this sequence will be repeated until the whistle is blown. On the whistle, the swimmers make their way down to the shallow end of the pool.

1 MINUTE REST

Training schedule

All participants swim front crawl.
a. Fartlek training
   Swim 400 metres:
      1st 25 metres slow speed
      2nd 25 metres ½ speed
      3rd 25 metres ¾ speed
   Repeat 5 times and finish with a slow length

1 MINUTE REST

b. Interval training
   a. pull 4 × 50 metres   15 seconds rest
   b. kick 6 × 50 metres   between each 50
   c. full stroke 4 × 50 metres metres

Take 30 seconds rest between each section and work at ¾ speed.

2 MINUTES REST

c. 'Catch-up' with hand paddles.
All participants swim continuously for 6 minutes using a 'catch-up' stroke. In this technique the starting position is with the arms extended along the water surface, close together and beyond the head. The swimmer then pulls and recovers with one arm and returns to the starting position; the swimmer then pulls and recovers the other arm. The extended position with both arms together is only held for a split second. It is essential that the swimmer kicks regularly to maintain a near-horizontal body position.

1 MINUTE REST

Variety

The participants select either back crawl or breast stroke. Swim 8 × 25 metres at ¾ speed. When the last swimmer in the lane has reached the end of the pool, the first swimmer starts the next length. The members of each lane should organise their own swimming order so that the faster ones, irrespective of stroke, should lead. If this is done correctly, swimmers do not get caught and there are no stoppages down the length.

Talk about the session

All participants should be encouraged to talk about the lesson. Did you:
- complete the schedule?
- manage the 'catch-up stroke?
- have enough rest between swims?
- find enough variety in the lesson?

A fitness lesson (enthusiast)

Plan

Objectives
Main teaching points
Equipment

Phase

Organisation
Warm up
Fitness: **a.** individual work
        b. pair work
Learn *or* improve: group work
Talk about the session

Approximate timing

Phases one and two should take one-fifth of the allocated time, phase three one-half, phase four one-fifth and phase five one-tenth.

Objectives
1. Complete the fitness schedule on back crawl or breast stroke or front crawl.
2. Spend time practising a turn relevant to your stroke.
3. Spend time practising the skill of treading water for two minutes continuously.
4. Train with others and discuss the session.

Plan

Main teaching points
General: 'stretch gently at the joints'
Strokes: back crawl – 'stretch the toes'
breast stroke – 'circle the feet' (kick)
front crawl – 'stretch the toes'
Turns: back crawl – 'touch with the flat hand' (spin turn)
breast stroke – 'look in the direction of the turn' (open turn)
front crawl – 'turn away from the touching arm' (throw-turn
Treading water: head position – 'keep the head back in the water'
arm action – 'scull with the hands close to the body'

Equipment
lane ropes
kick-boards
pull-buoys
clock with a sweep second hand

Phase

Organisation
a. Identify the swimmers' ability
b. Lanes:
 lane 1 – the weak swimmers
 lane 2 – good back crawlers with moderate front crawlers
 lane 3 – good front crawlers
 lane 4 – good breast strokers with moderate back crawlers
 lane 5 – use to ensure no lane is overcrowded.
c. Direction of swimming:
 lane 1 – clockwise
 lane 2 – anti-clockwise
 lane 3 – clockwise
 lane 4 – anti-clockwise
 lane 5 – clockwise.
d. Check that any adult swimmers are periodically examined by doctors and that they are fit enough to take part in the swimming lesson.

Warm up
All participants swim slowly and continuously and hold onto the lane rope or the side when they hear the whistle.
Can you:
- swim slowly on either breast stroke or life saving kick?

WHISTLE

- swim slowly on either back crawl or front crawl?

WHISTLE

- swim continuously and slowly alternating the stroke after each length? (use two strokes only)
- feel your ankles stretching in the crawl strokes?
- feel your feet turning out in the breast strokes?
- feel your shoulders loosening up?

Fitness

a. Individual work. All participants use their main stroke.

1. Swim full stroke

Can you:
- swim continuously?
- use a recognised turn at the end of each length?

2. Swim full stroke

Can you:
- swim repeated 1-lengths with a 10-second break between each at moderate speed? (e.g. 10 × 25 metres with 10 seconds rest)

WHISTLE

3. Can you:
- pull for two lengths, take a break of 20 seconds and keep repeating until you hear the whistle? (e.g. 5 × 50 metres with 20 seconds rest)

WHISTLE

b. Pair work

1. All participants practise kicking down the length with a partner. Pairs move off at five second intervals, and the first pair do not come back until the last pair has reached the end of the pool.

Can you:
- kick hard for the whole length?
- stay with your partner?
- catch the pair in front of you? (e.g. 10 × 25 metres at a good speed)

WHISTLE

2. All participants repeat the 1-length pair practice in full stroke.

WHISTLE

Improve

1. The participants are organised into small groups at both ends of each lane. The groups move 7 to 8 metres, away from the end walls, and members of each group practise, one at a time, a swimming turn.

Can you:
- go in at speed?
- stretch out of the turn?
- perform the turn without stopping at the wall?

WHISTLE

2. The participants all move into deep water in their respective lanes and practise treading water in their groups.
Can you:
- tread water for two or three minutes?
- change your leg kick?
- tread water with one arm behind your back?
- tread water with both arms behind your back?

WHISTLE

Talk about the session

All participants should be encouraged to talk about the lesson.
Did you:
- enjoy the lesson?
- find enough variety in the lesson?
- complete the schedule?
- improve your swimming turn?
- tread water for more than two minutes?
- have many unnecessary stoppages in your lane?
- feel that you had been placed in the right lane?

Index

Archimedes' principle 7
artificial aids 16–18

back crawl,
   arms 11, 38
   body position 37
   breathing 38
   legs 37
   teaching sequence 39–42
   timing 39
breathing 36
breast stroke,
   arms 11, 52–3
   body position 49
   breathing 53
   legs 50
   teaching sequence 54–7
   timing 53
buoyancy 7–9
   centre of buoyancy 7–9
butterfly dolphin,
   arms 11, 63–4
   body position 62
   breathing 65
   legs 62–3
   teaching sequence 65–9
   timing 65

competitive swimming 103–17

demonstrations 36
density 7–8
diving,
   early practices 73–7
   plain header 79–80
   plunge 78–9

elementary back stroke,
   arms 60
   body position 59
   breathing 60
   legs 60
   teaching sequence 60–2
   timing 60
expired air resuscitation 96–102

floating 87
front crawl,
   arms 11, 43
   body position 42–3
   breathing 44–5
   legs 42–3
   teaching sequence 46–9
   timing 46

game forms 26–9, 124–7
gliding 30, 34–5
gravity, centre of 7–9

hoop activities 29
hygiene 12–13

jumps,
   straddle 82
   straight 82
   tuck 82–3

lessons,
   confidence 128–30
   competitive
     swimming 137–39
   early stroke 131–33
   fitness 139–42
   water safety 134–36

life saving,
    problems   118–23
    reaching   91–5
    towing   94–5
    throwing   92–3
    wading   93
life saving kick,
    body position   57
    breathing   57
    legs   57
    teaching sequence   57–9

mushroom float   9

Newton's Laws of Motion   10

pool suitability   12
practices,
    arm   36
    ball   28
    confidence   22–6
    early diving   73–7
    early towing   95–6
    head under water   29, 34
    land   36
    loop   29

schedules   15–17
side stroke,
    arms   70
    body position   70
    breathing   70
    legs   70
    teaching sequence   71–2
    timing   70–1
starts,
    back stroke   105, 112
    front   103, 111
    grab   103–4, 111
    teaching sequence   111–12
supportive aids   31–2
survival in water,
    entry   81–3
    exits   89
    floating   87
    inflation of clothing   88–9
    swimming underwater   83–5
    submerging   83–5
    treading water   85–6

towing,
    bent arm chin   95
    cross chest   95
    extended arm chin   94
treading water   86
turns,
    back crawl spin   110, 115
    butterfly and breast
        stroke   105, 112
    teaching sequence   112–15
    throw-away   107
    tumble   108–9, 114
    twist and somersault   107–8, 113

water,
    cold   90–1
    fear of   20
    entry   22
    movement in   10–11
    open   15
    safety   14–15
    temperature   12
    walking in   22–4, 27–8